# TROUBLE SHOTS

GAME IMPROVEMENT LIBRARY™

# CREDITS

## TROUBLE SHOTS

**Tom Carpenter**
*Director of Book Development*

**Julie Cisler**
*Book Design & Production*

**Michele Teigen**
*Senior Book Development Coordinator*

**Steve Hosid**
*Instruction Editor/Photographer*

**Steve Ellis**
*Editor*

**Ward Clayton**      **Leo McCullagh**
**Bob Combs**        **Mike Mueller**
*PGA TOUR*

**Special thanks to the following golf courses for allowing us to shoot on location:**
The Tradition: La Quinta, California
TPC at Sawgrass: Ponte Vedra Beach, Florida
Arnold Palmer's Bay Hill Club & Lodge: Orlando, Florida
Preston Woods Golf Club: Dallas, Texas

**Acknowledgements**
"To the members of the PGA TOUR Partners Club I meet at tournaments around the country: Your questions, comments and support help create articles and books that truly reflect the needs of our outstanding membership."
—*Steve Hosid*

8 7 6 5 4 3 2 1 / 08 07 06 05 04 03 02 01
ISBN 1-58159-133-0
PGA TOUR Partners Club
12301 Whitewater Drive
Minnetonka, Minnesota 55343

## ABOUT THE AUTHOR/ PHOTOGRAPHER

**Steve Hosid** is instruction editor, contributing writer and photographer for *PGA TOUR Partners* magazine and the Club's Game Improvement Library. He is co-author of *The Complete Idiot's Guide to Healthy Stretching* (with Chris Verna), and *Golf for Everybody* (with Brad Brewer, former director of The Arnold Palmer Golf Academies), and has collaborated on books with LPGA star Michelle McGann and tennis player MaliVai Washington.

Steve is a graduate of the University of Southern California. He and his wife, Jill, live with two non-golfing Borzoi Wolfhounds on the 13th hole at Arnold Palmer's Bay Hill Club & Lodge in Orlando, Florida.

*PGA TOUR Partners Club President Tom Lehman (standing) with Steve Hosid.*

# CONTENTS

# INTRODUCTION

**T**rouble shots no longer are trouble shots once you learn how to play them. But try to force your normal technique and swing on shots requiring adjustments and improvisation, and you assuredly will pay the penalty.

Believe it or not, the world's best players have to deal with trouble shots too. Just *how* these TOUR professionals deal with trouble shots is part of what sets them apart and makes them great. When Tiger Woods won the *modern version* of the Grand Slam—holding at one time trophies from the Masters, U.S. and British Opens, PGA and THE PLAYERS Championship—his skill in dealing with trouble situations made the difference.

Getting out of trouble is just a part of the game!

Watch how meticulously the pros prepare to play from trouble. They begin by first assessing the difficulty and considering their various options. After committing to a specific remedy, they rehearse the shot several times, programming both their mind and body for the technique variations required and the associated feelings. Only then is the shot played *with a positive attitude*.

In trouble shot situations, it's true that there is no substitute for experience. But you have the next best thing in your hands right now to learn how to deal with those situations—four outstanding PGA TOUR players sharing their own experiences and techniques in an easy-to-follow format. You'll see many trouble shots and learn how to hit them properly.

Some of my closest friends in golf are in this book, and they really can help you. Past British Open champion Ian Baker-Finch works primarily as an analyst for ABC Sports and ESPN, but is getting back to playing. One of my more famous photos—seen on this page—features Ian, with his Claret Jug, and the late Payne Stewart, with the first of his two U.S. Open trophies, posing with Arnold Palmer. Both had won their major championships and were members of Arnold's Bay Hill Club & Lodge in Orlando, Florida.

Our other three pros—David Frost, Skip Kendall and Frank Lickliter—have all appeared in the pages of *Partners* magazine, providing game improvement tips for our members. Noted instructor Martin Hall and veteran PGA TOUR rules official Mark Russell also are part of the faculty. Martin's outstanding drills help you master various techniques, and Mark demonstrates how playing by The Rules of Golf can save unnecessary strokes.

While all of us can't keep you from getting into trouble, we are about to show you how to get yourself out of it correctly and effectively.

-Steve Hosid-

# MEET THE PLAYERS

## DAVID FROST

**Born:** September 11, 1959

**Height:** 5' 11" **Weight:** 190

**Turned Professional:** 1981

**Special Interests:** His award-winning David Frost Wines

10 PGA TOUR and 12 International victories, including three-time winner of the Million Dollar Challenge.

## IAN BAKER-FINCH

**Born:** October 24, 1960

**Height:** 6' 4" **Weight:** 190

**Turned Professional:** 1979

**Special Interests:** Golf-course design, fine wine and sports

1 PGA TOUR victory and 15 International titles, including 1991 British Open; commentator for ABC Sports and ESPN.

Like many young South African players, caddying for my father was my first exposure to the sport. Dad sold grapes that he raised, and I practiced by hitting balls in the vineyards, little suspecting that both would play such an important part of my future. By 17 I was a scratch handicap and later on was selected to represent my country in several international competitions. But being left out of one was my catalyst for turning pro.

I had to give up my job as a policeman, which was ideal since I had plenty of time to play and practice while still earning a paycheck. Fortunately, I won my first tournament in my second year as a pro.

I'll help you with sand play. Virtually any trouble shot you encounter, from fairway to greenside bunkers, can be successfully handled once you know how to adjust for the shot and know the correct technique to use.

*—David Frost*

Things other than the game fueled my interest in golf. My dad, along with a couple of guys in the area, received a grant to build a nine-hole course. Watching as they chopped down trees and started bonfires was great fun for a young lad of eight.

Hitting 9-irons between the sheds and the trees on our farm was great practice. I learned how to maneuver my hands and the clubface to my advantage. As a teenager, I used to play imaginary competitions against Arnold Palmer, Jack Nicklaus and Gary Player. I'd always win, too! Winning the British Open was the fulfillment of every Australian boy's dream.

I'll show you how to master some very demanding trouble shots. Photographed on the spectacular Tradition Course in California, it's the perfect venue for a wide variety of trouble shots you will encounter while playing today's modern courses.

*—Ian Baker-Finch*

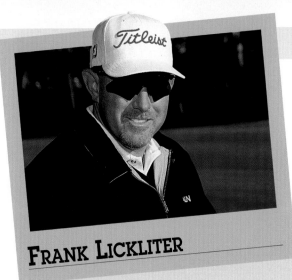

## FRANK LICKLITER

**Born:** July 28, 1969

**Height:** 6' 1" **Weight:** 200

**College:** Wright State University (Sociology)

**Special Interests:** Fishing, hunting and off-road excursions in his Hummer

Won 2001 Kemper Insurance Open; career low round of 62; once jumped over 50 positions on the money list six weeks after making adjustments in his setup.

## SKIP KENDALL

**Born:** September 9, 1964

**Height:** 5' 8" **Weight:** 150

**College:** University of Nevada-Las Vegas (Business Administration)

**Special Interests:** Family, reading, sports, rooting for the Green Bay Packers

Established himself as one of the TOUR's top-level players; has shot five rounds of 63 and recorded three runner-up finishes.

L ike most kids who grew up playing baseball and football, I considered golf an old man's sport. But when I took it up at 14, I was hooked. My dedication for working hard to improve at things showed up early in life.

I loved baseball and practiced every day by pitching against a square I had painted on a neighbor's concrete garage. My dad wouldn't let me throw anything but a fastball, and I became aware early on about the importance of target awareness by trying to hit the target every time.

The individual aspect of golf and relying just on yourself is one of the sport's most appealing aspects for me. I love being in the open spaces in absolutely beautiful surroundings and having the chance to see such a wide variety of wildlife.

Trouble shots are just one of those things golf throws at you. Professional golfers face trouble shots too, but years of practice help us understand how to handle them. In this book, I'll show you some of our techniques.

—*Frank Lickliter*

A t an early age my parents dragged me out to our local driving range. I couldn't hit a ball off the mat, so my parents, who were 25-handicappers, had the best of both worlds—keeping me occupied on one hand and being able to hit my balls, too.

I played college golf at UNLV. Fellow TOUR player Paul Goydos and I used to play a lot together. At best, we were average players. It's funny that a lot of the really good players at the time are not in the game now, but Paul and I are still playing. We worked very hard on our games, earning our right to play with the world's best golfers on the PGA TOUR.

We all face trouble shots, and the best way to handle them is being both realistic and determined. When a birdie is not reasonable from these situations, make up your mind that nothing will stop you from making par. For higher handicappers, set your goal as a bogey.

Demonstrating our techniques for playing some of the more difficult trouble shots you can encounter is only the first step toward successfully mastering them. You have to practice them too.

—*Skip Kendall*

**Martin Hall,** one of the game's top instructors, provides his proven practice drills throughout this book. Hall appears regularly on the PGA TOUR Partners Video Series and has been selected as one of the 50 best golf instructors in the U.S.

## MARTIN HALL

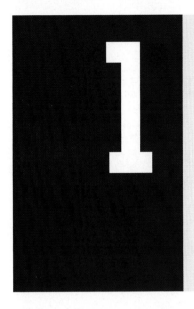

# 1

# ASK THE PROS

*"The difference between a sand bunker and water is the same as the difference between a car crash and an airplane crash. You have a chance of recovering from a car crash."—Bobby Jones*

**A**ll golfers face the daunting prospect of hitting trouble shots a few times during a round. Even our four featured PGA TOUR professionals sometimes find themselves in harm's way. If you wonder why such skilled players wind up in places assumed to be the exclusive territory of less proficient amateurs, the reason may very well be they actually hit a shot *too well.*

Being target oriented, pros work a ball's flight to land in a specific area of the fairway that provides the best chance for it to react in a certain manner. Sometimes the shot is shaped too much and, just like you, they need to get the ball back in play.

Our TOUR experts gather in this chapter for a question and answer session. They'll refer you to specific areas of the book to learn their trouble shot techniques. So pull up a chair as David, Ian, Frank and Skip give a professional's view on dealing with trouble shots.

*"Some of the best shots I remember hitting under pressure are shots from terrible lies."—Frank Lickliter*

# PRO: DAVID FROST

**QUESTION: SHOULD I USE THE SAME TECHNIQUE FOR SHOTS FROM A FAIRWAY BUNKER AS FROM A GREENSIDE BUNKER?**

## ANSWER:

The objective is different for both situations. Fairway bunkers require a distance-producing shot while getting the ball close to the pin is the goal from a greenside bunker. The key is to *pick* the ball out of a fairway bunker and *slide* the club under the ball from a greenside bunker.

Just telling you this doesn't help unless we couple it with instruction you can see. I'll show you the basic differences for both swings in Chapter 3. In the meantime, here's a brief explanation to get you started.

I usually take the club *inside* when playing from fairway bunkers and *outside* from greenside bunkers. Taking it inside allows me to create a longer swing, which produces more distance. Taking it outside limits my backswing for the shorter greenside bunker shot.

— *DAVID*

# PRO: IAN BAKER-FINCH

**QUESTION: "SHOULD I SHAPE THIS SHOT HIGH OR LOW?" WHAT'S THE SIMPLE RULE-OF-THUMB?**

## ANSWER:

Back home in Australia I learned early how much ball position meant to improvising a shot. Hitting for hours between the trees and sheds on our family farm helped me learn how to manipulate the clubhead to hit the exact trajectory needed to match any shot.

Simply put, if you want to hit a high shot, play the ball up in your stance and finish with your hands high. For the lower punch shots, invaluable for extricating yourself out of trouble, just the opposite is the case: Play the ball back in your stance and finish with your hands low.

Both techniques are shown and explained in Chapter 4. The keys: Don't change the tempo or timing of your swing. Only change ball position and how you finish.

— *IAN*

# PRO: FRANK LICKLITER

## QUESTION: WHAT CHANGES SHOULD I MAKE WHEN PLAYING IN THE WIND?

## ANSWER:

The day we shot pictures for the wind-play instruction in Chapter 7, the "breezes" howled at around 45 mph at the Tournament Players Club at Sawgrass. Whitecaps were even lapping the 18th fairway. Coupled with wind chill temperatures below 25 degrees, you will find an honest depiction of wind play in this book!

I love the wind because growing up in southwestern Ohio, we had a lot of it during the spring and fall. Understanding wind play turns what some players may think is a trouble shot into an advantage for me.

I'll show you how to tailor your game to work with the wind instead of being victimized by it. It does require a little more imagination. In Chapter 7 we cover wind-affected shots from a variety of distances.

— *FRANK*

# PRO: SKIP KENDALL

## QUESTION: HOW MUCH BACKSWING SHOULD I TAKE WHEN A TREE IS IN THE CLUB'S PATH?

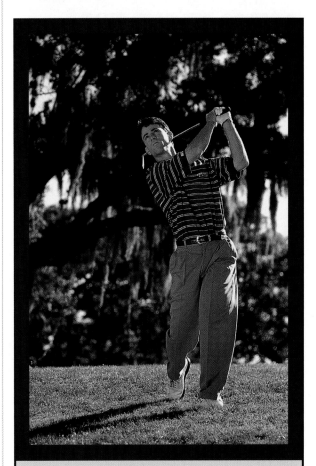

## ANSWER:

Look at every option available, including getting down on your knees to play the shot. My first decision, though, is choosing where my next shot should be played from and how I can get the ball there from this situation.

Mark Russell provides some rules for tree obstructions in Chapter 8. Keeping those in mind, I'll show you several variations of blocked tree shots from 100 yards in Chapter 4. As you'll see, sometimes changing the backswing angle (by picking the club up and setting the wrist angle early) helps you escape the tree's branches.

— *SKIP*

# PRO: DAVID FROST

## QUESTION: HOW SHOULD I PLAY A GREENSIDE BUNKER SHOT WHEN THE BALL IS SO CLOSE TO THE FACE THAT I CAN'T FOLLOW THROUGH?

## ANSWER:

The answer is similar to the question "what's the best way to get to Carnegie Hall?" Rehearse, rehearse and rehearse! Seriously, though, depending on how close you are to the bunker face, there are a number of ways to play the shot.

I'll show you different techniques in Chapter 6. The key, however, is to determine if you can get to the ball and through it without slamming the club into the face of the bunker. If you are on an upslope, positioning your shoulders parallel to the slope allows the club to swing along an upward plane, which should allow you to clear the lip.

How do you know for sure? Before playing your shot, rehearse like we do. Explore your options!

— *DAVID*

# PRO: IAN BAKER-FINCH

## QUESTION: WHAT ADVICE CAN YOU GIVE ME WHEN MY LIE DOES NOT ALLOW ME TO SEE THE PIN?

## ANSWER:

If your mind does not know where the shot is supposed to go, you are not going to hit a very good shot. So always be sure you have a specific target to aim toward.

Sometimes you may find yourself in a gully or blocked by some other obstruction that does not allow a clear view of the green. Chapter 2 provides some helpful answers to help you get out of that mild trouble shot safely.

A golf course is filled with helpful solutions … when you think of a canvas stretched behind the green. I'll show you how I might "target" a boulder on a mountain, the top of a tree or a cloud in the sky.

— *IAN*

# PRO: FRANK LICKLITER

QUESTION: SOME OF THE TOUGHEST TROUBLE SHOTS ARE FROM THE ROUGH. ANY SUGGESTIONS ON HOW TO CUT DOWN ON STROKES?

## ANSWER:

Chapter 2 features a section on what to do when facing various long shots from the rough, and Chapter 4 demonstrates playing wedges from the rough. I'll show you how to chip with your ball against the collar in Chapter 5.

One of the first things to observe when you survey a shot from the rough is this: What direction is the grass growing? Is it growing with the shot or against it? Use that thought for selecting the correct club.

I'll also show you how ball position relative to your stance plays a role in the type of shot you'll need. This simple tip creates the proper attack angle as the club makes its descent. I use slightly different techniques if the ball is sitting on top of or at the bottom of the rough.

— *FRANK*

# PRO: SKIP KENDALL

QUESTION: DO I GET ANY RELIEF WHEN MY BALL LANDS IN A DIVOT?

## ANSWER:

PGA TOUR rules official Mark Russell explains in Chapter 8 which of three divot-affected shots you can get free relief from. The other two situations require playing the shot from where it lies.

I'll demonstrate playing from these fairway divots in Chapter 3. The real key is playing the shot using the same technique David demonstrates for playing out of fairway bunkers. Hit the ball first!

Even if a divot is filled, you don't know how deep the divot is, as Payne Stewart frustratingly discovered during the 1998 U.S. Open.

— *SKIP*

# PRO: DAVID FROST

### QUESTION: WHAT TIPS CAN YOU GIVE ME WHEN I HAVE TO STAND ON THE GRASS TO HIT THE BALL OUT OF THE BUNKER, OR STAND IN THE BUNKER TO HIT THE BALL FROM THE GRASS?

### ANSWER:

The key to these trouble shots is adjusting the height of your shoulders to compensate for the difference between the lies.

As I'll show you in Chapter 6, the primary key is adjusting the height of your shoulders. For shots where the ball is lower than my feet, I don't bend at the waist to get closer. I widen my stance instead, naturally bringing my shoulders closer to the ball.

Maintaining a solid lower body while playing trouble shots from a sloping bunker terrain is another of the points I'll demonstrate. All of my experiences hitting from bunkers are available to you in Chapter 6.

### — DAVID

# PRO: IAN BAKER-FINCH

### QUESTION: HOW DO YOU PLAY SHOTS FROM THE ROCKS?

### ANSWER:

Mark Russell explains some of your options in Chapter 8. With all the desert courses available for play, facing some rocky trouble shots occurs if you hit a wayward drive or miss a green by 10 to 15 yards. Most of the time the soil is sandy between the rocks.

I'll show you my preferences for playing these shots in Chapter 7. Here's a brief tip: For shorter shots, I play it as I would from the sand, with an explosion shot. If I need to create a shot to gain more distance, I'll pick it off the surface, making sure to hit the ball first before contacting the ground.

### — IAN

# PRO: FRANK LICKLITER

## QUESTION: IF A TREE IS IN MY PATH, SHOULD I HIT THE BALL OVER OR UNDER THE TREE?

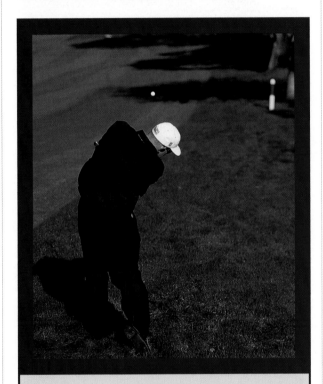

## ANSWER:

That all depends. The one thing you should always have is an open mind. Don't make up your mind as to what type of shot to play until you have studied the situation and your options.

I may also choose to shape the shot around the tree. I'll show you my technique for shot shaping in Chapter 2. A fade is my normal shot (a ball that moves from left-to-right for a right-hander), but when the situation calls for it I can bend it the other way. The more shots you have in your bag, the better player you will be.

One tip: If you are riding in a cart, always take more than one club when you walk to your ball. Since you really don't know which shot you'll actually play until you survey the situation, avoid the common mistake of not being able to play the correct shot because you didn't bring the proper club.

— *FRANK*

# PRO: SKIP KENDALL

## QUESTION: CAN I EVER PLAY A BACKWARD SHOT TO ESCAPE TROUBLE?

## ANSWER:

Yes, and I'll show you how in Chapter 4. On more than a few occasions, I've turned my sand wedge upside down and played shots like Phil Mickelson, as a left-hander.

During the course of a round, the chances of playing this shot may be slim—which is a good thing—but I practice it just in case it comes up during a tournament. We can demonstrate the techniques for all of these trouble shots, but the only way to master them is to take the information and practice.

Then, the next time you're playing a match with your buddies and find yourself with a troublesome lie, you can pull the shot off just like a pro.

— *SKIP*

# 2 LONG GAME TROUBLE

*"If a great-looking golf swing puts you high on the money list, there'd be some of us who would be broke."*—Raymond Floyd

**W**hile teeing your ball, your shot was properly visualized in your mind, the targeted landing area was selected and the trajectory to reach it was locked and loaded. All you had to do was pull the trigger and triumphantly march down the fairway toward golfing glory.

Unfortunately, golf is a game played on the ground, and even well-struck balls sometimes take wayward bounces. Of course, that's giving you the benefit of the doubt that everything back on the tee was handled with the utmost skill and precision. In any event, your next shot must be played from a less-than-perfect lie. Such is golf; such is life.

Our troubleshooters for this chapter are British Open champion and ABC-TV golf analyst Ian Baker-Finch, and Frank Lickliter. PGA TOUR rules official Mark Russell offers suggestions, based on the rules, to avoid a trouble lie on the tee and penalty strokes from awkward stance positions along the way. And Martin Hall's drills will strive to eliminate any trouble before it begins.

*"If you hit every shot on the sweetspot, normally the ball ends up in pretty good position. Sometimes, though, it ends up in a nasty position, and then you have to look at that as a challenge."*—Frank Lickliter

# TROUBLE SAVER:
# AVOIDING TROUBLE OFF THE TEE

This book's goal is to teach you how to get out of trouble, but we'll never shy away from pointing out a few things that can help you keep from getting into trouble in the first place.

In that vein, our first two suggestions—dubbed "Trouble Savers"—deal with avoiding trouble off the tee. Specifically, they cover planning your tee shot to stay away from the trouble, and then tips on teeing up the ball.

## AVOIDING REACHABLE HAZARDS

PGA TOUR professionals carefully evaluate each situation before teeing up their ball. Past experience with terrain and weather, coupled with hazard awareness, are factored into choosing the landing target before the club is pulled from the bag. With the target firmly in mind, the shot is visualized and then executed without hesitation or trepidation.

Less skilled golfers tend to focus only on the trouble, and invariably that's where they'll end up. Even worse is not factoring in the potential trouble and playing the shot regardless of the outcome.

Golf is a game of stroke elimination. Failing to avoid trouble when you had the chance can add a bundle of strokes instead of eliminating them.

## POOR TEE BOX CONDITIONS

The tee boxes of some courses often show the wear and tear of extensive play (inset below), especially between the tee markers. Look behind the markers for better ground to tee your ball.

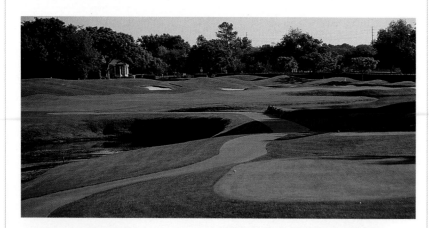

### TOUR TIPS

1 Plan your shot to avoid the trouble.

2 If your present skill level allows you to work the ball, hit a fade away from the trouble or start a draw far enough away so that it can't reach the trouble as it curves back.

3 Select a club that offers more precision or won't let you reach the trouble in the first place.

### KNOW THE RULES

The Rules of Golf allow you to tee your ball two club-lengths back anywhere within the markers.—*Mark Russell*

# IAN'S BASIC AIMING ADJUSTMENTS

Before playing a shot from a lie above or below your feet, adjust your address position and clubhead alignment to compensate for that shot's particular tendency. The ball will not fly straight to the target. It will draw or fade depending on your lie.

*BALL BELOW YOUR FEET*

*BALL ABOVE YOUR FEET*

Ball takes this path

Target

With the ball below your feet, follow this checklist to compensate for a naturally occurring fade (left-to-right ball flight for a right-hander):

✔ Select an aiming target more to the left of your real target.

✔ Align your body position parallel to your aiming target.

✔ As the ball flies, it will curve back toward your real target.

✔ The steeper the slope, the more the ball will fade, so compensate accordingly.

When the ball is above your feet, follow this checklist to compensate for a naturally occurring draw (right-to-left ball flight for a right-hander):

✔ Select an aiming target more to the right of your real target.

✔ Align your body position parallel to the aiming target.

✔ As the ball flies, it will curve back toward your real target.

✔ The steeper the slope, the more the ball will draw, so compensate accordingly.

# TROUBLE SHOT:
# BALL BELOW YOUR FEET

As you look at the large photo on this page, notice how balanced I am at impact despite the severe downward sloping of my lie. This balance is still in force (inset) as I follow through to gain maximum distance.

Along with setting yourself up more to the left of your real target to allow for the natural fade, I have some tips that will help you consistently master this shot.

But first here's a simple way to remember which way the ball will naturally curve. Its natural arc will be in the direction of the lowest part of the slope. If the ball is below your feet, it will curve to the low side, or left-to-right. If the ball is above your feet, it will still curve to the low side, but in this case the flight will be right-to-left. (Left-handers will find the ball flights will be reversed, but they will always be toward the low side.)

*FOLLOW-THROUGH IN BALANCE*

# IAN'S BALANCE KEYS

Gravity tries to bring you forward down the hill, so it's imperative to build a steady base. The ball is at least a foot below where it would be in a normal lie, so here's my compensation to get lower: Widen your stance.

## IAN SAYS:

Always have a clear picture of what you are going to do before you get into the shot. That takes on more importance with trouble shots. Begin by standing behind your ball, deciding on what you are going to do, selecting the club, visualizing the shot you are committed to hitting and then stepping into it and executing.

### WIDEN YOUR STANCE

**Normal Stance**

**Widened Stance**

*I widen my stance, instead of bending forward at the waist, to get lower to the ball. This accomplishes two important things:*

- *I can hold this solid base position throughout my swing, enhancing my balance.*

- *The compensation allows me to set the bottom of my swing arc by adjusting my shoulders downward. I'm still at the same relative height I would be from a flat lie, so there's no need to grip down on the club.*

# TROUBLE SHOT:
# BALL ABOVE YOUR FEET

Your first consideration when playing this trouble shot is realizing you are in trouble with the potential to get into even deeper trouble. Don't bite off more than you can chew.

Even though I'm 200 yards away, I might take a 7-iron if the slope were too severe. Reaching the green with my third shot from a closer and level lie in the fairway should get me near enough to convert the par.

Forcing a shot could send me into some of the more beautiful and colorful areas here on The Tradition. Beauty is in the eye of the beholder, and I would much rather be on the beautiful short green stuff instead of in the wildflowers or desert brush.

### COMMIT TO THE SHOT

*My back is facing my target, illustrating my total commitment to this 200-yard shot. I'll demonstrate some balance compensations and stance adjustments on the next page.*

# IAN'S ADJUSTMENTS

Earlier you learned that shots with the ball above your feet must be aimed and set up to the right of your actual target. The natural tendency is for the ball to follow a right-to-left hooking arc. Hand extension coming through as the club is closing easily will help you turn that into a high draw.

Another compensation is adjusting your posture to match a ball that is now at least a foot higher than it would be in a normal lie. My compensation is the narrowing of my stance to make me taller.

*EXTEND THROUGH THE SWING*

*Extending your swing arc through the shot turns a hook into a high draw.*

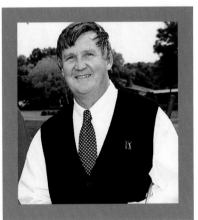

## KNOW THE RULES

Have you ever noticed that Jack Nicklaus never soles his club prior to making a shot. The reason is the penalty stroke you would have to call on yourself should the ball inadvertently move, which increases in probability with trouble lies.

If you take your stance but don't sole your club, no penalty situation has occurred.—*Mark Russell*

*NARROW YOUR STANCE*

**Normal Stance**

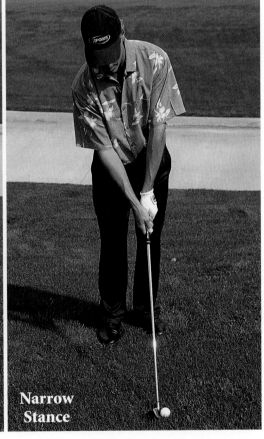

**Narrow Stance**

*I narrow my stance to get my shoulders higher to the ball. I can hold this solid base position throughout my swing, enhancing my balance. Always adjust your body to the lie instead of just choking down on the club. Shortening costs you distance and does nothing to improve your swing balance.*

# TROUBLE SHOT:
# UPHILL, DOWNHILL LIES

The trouble faced from these lies is clear: One causes the ball to go higher while the other fights getting the ball airborne. Setup adjustments, along with some tweaking of technique, help master both these trouble situations.

Keep this positive thought uppermost in your mind: If you hit a good drive down the middle of the fairway and catch a bad break, you can still fight for a good score on the hole if you find some positive element in every unfortunate situation. Here are Ian Baker-Finch's suggestions for playing these shots.

## BALL ON UPSLOPE

A couple of things to watch out for when facing this situation: the ball is going to want to go higher as a result of the slope; and you'll have difficulty following through because your weight is behind the shot.

*1- DETERMINE SETUP ANGLES* | *2- TAKE MORE CLUB* | *3- BALANCE YOUR FOLLOW-THROUGH*

*When you have a sloping shot, set the angle of your shoulders to the slope of the hill you're dealing with. Your attack angle will naturally want to take the ball up the slope, launching it higher than normal, so you need Step 2 to compensate for that situation.*

*If the shot distance called for a 7-iron I may take a 5-iron from the same distance. This lowers the shot's trajectory, combating the ball's natural tendency to fly high and stop quickly.*

*Rehearsing your swing on the slope ahead of time helps keep you in balance for the real swing. Tempo is important for shots like these, so don't rush your swing.*

# BALL ON DOWNSLOPE

This lie fights the ball getting into the air, and you'll make it even worse by trying to help it get airborne. This leads to fat shots instead of the distance-producing shot you need to keep in the hunt for a good score. Downslopes make you feel as if you're falling forward. Here are some steps to help your balance, follow-through and shotmaking.

### 1- SET YOUR ANGLES TO THE SLOPE

*Just the opposite of the upslope shot, your shoulders, hips and knees (dotted lines) should be set parallel to the downslope angle. Instead of trying to lift the ball in the air, your club selection and ball placement take on that responsibility.*

### 2- TAKE LESS CLUB

*If you take less club, your 7-iron instead of your 5-iron for example, the extra loft goes to work for you. Place the ball back in your stance, optimizing a downward angle of attack for the extra loft offered by the 7-iron. The ball will most likely land short of the green and run on. If you used the 5-iron, the slope would close the club to 3-iron loft, which makes getting the ball airborne difficult (or even impossible for some golfers).*

### 3- GARY PLAYER WALK-THROUGH

*Gary Player finishes most of his shots by walking through the finish, ensuring his weight transferred correctly. Shifting your weight down the hill is simple, but controlling it through your shot to optimize distance is another story. Maintain a normal weight transfer, but don't try to hold your finish position. Instead, allow yourself to walk through the finish like Gary.*

Long
Game
Trouble

# TROUBLE SHOT:
# IN THE ROUGH

Any time you have a shot from the rough, you have to determine how much grass is going to get between the ball and clubface. In other words: How much club can you get on the ball?

I'm powering through this shot with a more lofted club because the ball was down deep. You encounter less resistance for some shots because the grass is growing in the direction you want the ball to go, or the ball is sitting up.

PGA TOUR events are a real test of a pro's skills and creativity because we encounter several different cuts of rough. I've chosen four different situations to cover. All are fairly common on many private and municipal courses.

When the USGA sets up a U.S. Open course, they want a penal rough. If you land in the tall stuff, they want it to cost you. The bottom line is to be realistic with your expectations once you land in the rough.

# FRANK'S ROUGH EXAMPLES

On the upcoming pages, we'll talk about how to deal with several types of shots from the rough. But first, it's worth analyzing and understanding what you're dealing with in each situation. You'll see these examples below.

### 1A- FIRST CUT ON TOP

### 1B- FIRST CUT BURIED LIE

The first type of rough—the first cut—actually has two variations: with the ball on top (photo 1A) and a buried lie (photo 1B). Pages 28 and 29 show you how to deal with these shots.

*You'll encounter this shot when your drive rolls just through the fairway and onto this low cut of rough.*

*Technically it's a missed fairway, but the ball sits up so beautifully that the shot should not cause you difficulty. In fact, it may be easier to play than a tight fairway lie!*

*Not much grass will get between the clubface and the ball, so creating backspin is not a problem.*

*If you encounter this trouble shot, your ball came down steeply from a high trajectory.*

*Because of the lie, you have to go down and get it. I'll show you how to do just that and send the ball on a target path toward the green.*

### 2- DEEP ROUGH WITH THE GRAIN

### 3- DEEP ROUGH AGAINST THE GRAIN

*The ball is in the deep stuff but the grass is growing in the same direction the ball must go. This is still trouble but we should be able to get the club on the ball.*

*This is the tough one. The grass is growing against the direction the ball needs to go, so resistance is the operative word. We'll have to go down and through for this one!*

The second type of rough is the deep rough. Consider yourself fortunate if your swing will be *with* the grass's grain (photo 2). Pages 30 and 31 show you how to deal with this shot.

There's a much more challenging version of the deep rough shot, and photo 3 shows it: a deep rough where you have to shoot *against* the grass's grain (photo 3). Pages 32 and 33 show you how to work this shot successfully.

# TROUBLE SHOT:
# ROUGH FIRST CUT

Your skill level must increase the farther and deeper down you get in the rough. Club selection plays a role. Pulling the correct club depends on the ball's position in the rough and the direction the grass is growing.

Better players can control the distance they hit the ball, and it's reaction after landing, if the clubface is able to impact the ball against the bare grooves. Once you introduce grass between those two surfaces, the amount of backspin created will be affected and so will the distance and the trajectory. A ball leaving any cut of rough with less back-spin than normal is called a flyer because a lot of what it's going to do is unknown.

### ON THE SURFACE

*This is just a regular shot. The clubface will impact the ball with little if any interference from the grass. The picture is shown to help you distinguish between various problems and techniques.*

*That's not to say this shot is without its own trouble. Should the ball move inadvertently once you address it, the rules state you must assess yourself one penalty stroke. In Chapter 8, Mark Russell offers his insurance policy advice on what to do in situations like this to eliminate the possibility of a penalty stroke.*

### FIRST CUT BURIED LIE

*This is a trouble shot. The ball is buried only in the grass, so you are not entitled to replace, per The Rules of Golf. Here's how I set up to play this shot, limiting the amount of grass between the ball and the clubface:*

*Set up with the ball back in your stance. This ball position encourages the club to descend with a steeper attack angle. A steeper attack limits the amount of intrusive grass as the ball is popped out of its lie.*

### BACKSWING UNDER CONTROL

*Here's why a professional's hand-eye coordination is so much better than that of less skilled players: We do things slowly while they do them fast. The slower the club is moving, the more you can feel it. My controlled backswing will allow me to return the clubface to the ball position.*

# SOLUTION: STEEP ANGLE OF ATTACK

With the ball back in my stance, the descending clubhead will impact the ball before taking a divot. The amount of material that gets trapped between the face and the ball should be limited with this technique. The downward angle of a lofted club pops the ball up and down the line toward the green.

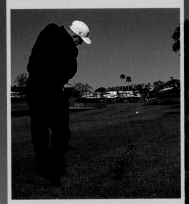

### DOWN AND OUT

*Going down for the ball works in this situation. The clubhead contacted the ball before taking the divot you see in this photo.*

### FOLLOW-THROUGH

*Never quit on a shot, especially those hit from trouble lies. You must finish for the technique to work. Should you quit early, the ball will never go the direction or distance you need.*

*Here, my ball is on its way toward the hole. With less backspin than normal, the ball will release and roll, which I planned for with my club selection.*

Long
Game
Trouble

# TROUBLE SHOT:
# DEEP ROUGH
# WITH THE GRAIN

**GRASS GROWING IN THE DIRECTION OF THE SHOT**

*The one bright light in this trouble situation is that the growth is toward the hole. My trusty 8-iron is the club I usually go with when my ball is in deep rough like this. But with the grass growth in the direction of the shot, even a 4-iron may work. When grass grows with your shot, the clubhead encounters less resistance than if the grass were growing toward the ball.*

### BALL BACK IN STANCE

### ABBREVIATED FINISH

*I want my shot to go 150 to 160 yards from this deep rough lie. The key is playing the ball back in my stance and swinging through steeply and aggressively.*

### EXTEND THROUGH THE SHOT

*The clubhead should easily slip through longer grass that grows in the direction of the shot. Obtain the maximum distance by making a good tempo swing and extending through the shot.*

*Notice my follow-through position is not around my back. The steeper downswing and impact with the ground will limit the amount of momentum you have going through. However, I'm facing the target.*

# TROUBLE SHOT:
# DEEP ROUGH
# AGAINST THE GRAIN

The best advice I can give should you face this trouble shot is to swing steeper, not harder. It will be tough, but get down to the ball, trapping as little grass as possible between the clubface and ball.

You need to grip the club a little tighter to keep the face from closing down. Sometimes, though, no matter how perfectly you set up or how well you swing at it, the rough is still going to grab your clubface.

## FRANK'S DEEP ROUGH TIPS

Your starting point for deep rough trouble lies can be modified once the situation has clearly been thought out. Maybe it's my hunting background, but analyzing trouble shots is a lot like stalking your prey. You are faced with having to do something regardless of whether it's right or wrong. Patience in golf or hunting is vital to the outcome. Paying attention to minute details and looking for every advantage leads to success.

## CLUB AND BALL POSITION

My 8-iron can get me out of almost any lie unless it's absolutely terrible, and then I have to drop down to a wedge.

Play the ball back in your stance to encourage a steeper downward angle of attack.

Resign yourself to the fact that you aren't likely to reach the green from this lie. Play just to get back in a position where you have a chance to get up and down.

You must be aggressive to power the ball out of this horrible lie. I'm not bringing the club back to parallel, but I'm loading power behind the ball with a full backswing. When I release, the swing will be in tempo to allow all the timing elements to come together at impact. I'm not swinging harder or faster, but I'm swinging steeper.

## CLEAR THE HIPS

### FINISH FACING YOUR TARGET

This downswing photo illustrates how my hips have cleared out of the way, allowing room for my arms, hands and club to swing powerfully through the ball. Just as with full swings, your hips begin the transition to the downswing.

My clubhead powered through the grass and freed the ball from this deep lie (1). My weight has transferred over to the left side and I finish facing my target (2).

Long
Game
Trouble

33

# TROUBLE SHOT:
# CAN'T SEE THE TARGET

The Tradition is one of the most beautiful courses I've ever played. Designed by Arnold Palmer, it's located in La Quinta, California, a suburb of Palm Springs. The sloping of the fairways and greens is often spectacular but, on occasion, presents a problem you may have on your own course.

The green is not visible from this fairway hollow. Even a tall guy like me, standing on my tiptoes or jumping up (see small photo), can't pick out the green. This is a problem, because if your mind doesn't know where to hit the ball, you're not going to hit a good shot. You need to have a clear target.

Fortunately, the magnificent mountain behind the green is nature's backdrop, offering not only beauty but also target selection. When you're faced with a similar situation, walk up to a point in the fairway and pick out a target you'll be able to see that is aligned with the pin. It may be a treetop or a slow-moving cloud.

*Walking up the hill allows you to align a spot in the background (target) with your real target. Mine is the outcropping on the mountain ridge.*

# PRACTICE TEE

Trouble shots from uneven lies may lack the "star quality" of a behind-a-tree save, but chances are you'll encounter them more often during a typical round. Stay in control of the situation by incorporating these suggestions into your technique for playing them.

## UPHILL LIES

Uphill shots tend to fly higher, so compensate by switching to a less lofted club. Two other tips will help:

• Open your stance to help your hips turn through the shot.

• Swing up the slope, not into it.

*OPEN STANCE*

1

2

With such a slanted, off-balance stance, it's hard to get your lower body through uphill shots with your normal foot alignment (1). The solution is opening up your stance by bringing your left foot back from the line (2).

## PRACTICE SWINGING UP THE SLOPE

Uneven stances require programming your mind for feel, balance and technique. Stand back from your ball and practice swinging up the slope; try to sense your balance points.

*PRACTICE SETUP/IMPACT*

*Practicing impact as you swing up the slope allows you to correctly determine the bottom of your swing arc, ensuring solid contact. You should not take a divot, so adjust your ball position accordingly as you take your stance.*

*PRACTICE BACKSWING*

*The weight begins on the back foot. As you practice swinging up the slope, you'll find it should stay on that back foot. Do not rush your swing: Timing and tempo are both important elements for success.*

*PRACTICE FOLLOW-THROUGH*

*When you swing up the contour of the slope, you will find your weight remains on your back foot.*

Long
Game
Trouble

# DOWNSLOPE

The basic plan for playing this shot is to set your shoulders parallel to the downslope and use a more lofted club. The more lofted clubface will naturally close down to about the same loft of your normal club selection as you take your stance. Then adjust your stance and "walk down the slope" to master this shot.

*STANCE ADJUSTMENTS*

*The ball is played back in my stance. I also want to keep all my weight on my left or downhill side throughout the swing so I roll my right foot over onto its instep (inset photo).*

*WALK DOWN THE SLOPE*

*A few practice swings instill the correct feelings for playing this downhill lie shot. I want the club to follow the downslope to avoid trying to help the ball into the air. The practice impact position (1) helps determine the correct ball position. I add one unique ingredient to my follow-through (2): I follow the shot down the hill (3) just like the legendary golfer Henry Cotton.*

# BALL ABOVE THE FEET

How you aim is a big consideration whenever you face a shot with the ball above your feet. Unless you compensate, the ball will go left of your target, especially with more lofted clubs.

### SHOT WILL BE LEFT

*A magnetic pointer shows the clubface position at address (1). As I hold it up to represent the swing (2), notice how far it points downhill. Compensate by aiming more uphill.*

### SWING LEVEL

*Take a few practice swings, keeping the club about waist high to develop a feeling for a level swing. The weight should be more on your toes.*

# BALL BELOW THE FEET

### PIGEON-TOED

*When the ball is below your feet, compensations must be made to help maintain your balance. As with all these uneven lie shots, the goal is making solid contact with the ball.*

*I find standing pigeon-toed helps provide some additional balance restriction to prevent falling forward as I swing for balls below my feet.*

### RESTRICTED LOWER BODY

*Standing pigeon-toed and keeping more weight on my heels (inset) restricts my lower body movement. The key to this shot is making solid contact and getting the ball back in play from this trouble lie.*

# 3 MID-COURSE CORRECTIONS

*"You must be committed to the shot. Know what you want to do before you hit it. Visualize where the ball is going to end up."—Skip Kendall*

Fairway divots, fairway bunkers and trees are some of the trouble shots encountered along the way of a round of golf. They must be handled properly or your score balloons.

Golf history is filled with recollections of great championship-saving shots. Sadly, it's also replete with occurrences where championships were lost from trouble situations, as Payne Stewart discovered at the 1998 U.S. Open. Payne had the championship in his grasp until his ball settled in a filled divot on The Olympic Club's 18th hole. And he knew how to play the shot!

Perfect execution does not always result in perfect trouble shots, but implementing the correct technique increases your odds for success. Turning the ball flight at your will, controlling its trajectory and picking it off the sand are some of the tricks of the trade you'll learn from Skip Kendall, David Frost and Frank Lickliter in this chapter.

*"Palm Springs has a lot of golf courses, and President Ford doesn't know which course he'll play until after his first tee shot."—Scott Hoch*

# Trouble Shot:
# Hitting Out of a Divot

Even the best of drives can end up in another player's divot. Even if they replaced or filled it, you're still facing a trouble shot. If the divot is unfilled at least you know how deep it is. But if it's filled with loose sand or dirt, its depth is a mystery.

Play out of a divot like it's a fairway bunker shot—hitting the ball before the ground. If you contact the ground first, the ball will not react very well. Here's Skip Kendall's method for success.

### BALL POSITION

*Position the ball slightly back in the stance. I move mine back about half a ball length, as you see in the comparison photo.*

### CHOKE DOWN

*Slightly choke down on the grip. To compensate for any loss of distance as a result, take one club more: If it's 5-iron distance, take a 4-iron.*

### LESS THAN FULL SWING

*You want a level swing to play this trouble shot, so my backswing is similar to a knockdown shot. The backswing does not have to reach parallel.*

# LEVEL YOUR SWING

A level swing that makes solid contact with the ball *before* taking a divot is the goal. My key is to set the club with my right shoulder high, which enables me to stay level. If the shoulders or head dip anytime during the swing, a fat shot will be the result.

In the large photo you can clearly see that my divot is more than halfway through the old divot, indicating I struck the ball first.

### DOWNSWING

*My lower body is square to the target line as I pull the club down. Notice how level my shoulders are while turning toward the ball.*

### FOLLOW-THROUGH

*My shoulders remained level even at follow-through. This will not be a high shot, but the ball will travel the distance needed to reach the green. I couldn't avoid this trouble, but I handled it properly.*

## KNOW THE RULES

There's one type of divot you can get relief from without a penalty stroke. We'll cover it in Chapter 8. In Skip's situation, he has to play the shot where it lies.—*Mark Russell*

# FAIRWAY BUNKERS

Finding yourself in a fairway bunker does not rule out making a good score on the hole. The first thing all golfers must do is think positively about the situation. This may be a trouble shot. But once you understand the basics that go into long sand play, you will have the confidence to pull it off.

To begin, get it clear in your mind, as you approach your ball, that to make a good score on the hole your next shot from the fairway bunker needs two elements—**escape plus distance.** It's not enough to pop the ball out of the bunker, leaving yourself yet another long shot to the green.

This is accomplished by *not* making the same swing as you do from a greenside bunker. The reason is, you want **to pick the ball** out of fairway bunkers, as I have in the photo, and **explode the ball** out of greenside bunkers. Two different approaches that require two different swings.

# BASIC FAIRWAY BUNKER PLAY

Remember that, as you prepare to play your shot from a fairway bunker, the entire setup will be geared toward **escape plus distance**. The first consideration is which club to use.

- Always use one club more than you would use from the same distance on the fairway.

- You can't exert the same amount of force out of a fairway bunker as you can out of a normal fairway lie or in the rough.

- You need to clip the ball without taking a lot of sand, so the swing will be a little softer. Selecting an extra club provides the extra confidence you need to slow your swing down.

## OPEN THE CLUBFACE

*NORMAL*

To handle the **escape** portion of our equation, we need to create loft for the shot. Slightly opening your clubface before gripping the club accomplishes this, but we'll have to compensate for this at address. You can see the difference in the photos.

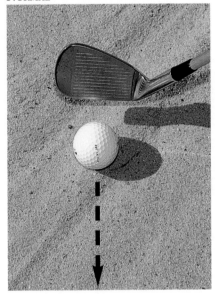

*Normal clubface position.*

*OPEN*

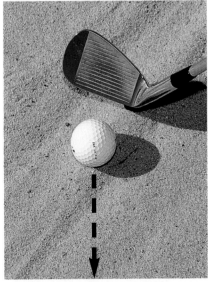

*Slightly opened clubface position.*

## ADDRESS COMPENSATIONS

**You must aim left of the target**. This will compensate for the club being open at address (remember, you have opened the clubface to increase loft). One of the main reasons fairway bunker shots cause problems is due to incorrectly aiming right of the target and closing the clubface. Poor shots result because the club will come over the ball instead of sweeping through and picking it off the sand.

*My club is slightly open and I'm aiming left of the target line.*

*Moving my left foot back from the target line creates the open stance I'll need to clear my body through the shot.*

# PICK THE BALL OUT OF FAIRWAY BUNKERS

Picking your way out of a fairway bunker produces escape and distance. The key to accomplish this is to stay on a normal up-and-around swing plane instead of the shorter, more upright greenside bunker swing.

Compare the photos on these two pages to see the most visible difference before I demonstrate the actual swing.

The wide swing arc that brought the club back from the ball creates the distance I need to play this shot successfully. I'll continue to the top, making a complete backswing, before starting down.

The key difference in both of these shots is the club's position. The butt of the club is pointed between the target line and my stance line for this distance-producing swing. This is the same way it points for my normal full swings.

My stance is aimed to the left of my target line.

*A clean pick! Only a wisp of sand is visible after impact.*

# EXPLODE OUT OF GREENSIDE BUNKERS

Becoming a good fairway bunker player requires abandoning the greenside bunker mentality of a short, more upright swing. You need length, not a short, soft landing shot.

David Frost points out the difference in the two positions. Chapter 5 is dedicated to greenside bunker play.

Instead of the wider, more up-and-around swing arc you see on page 44, this greenside bunker position shows a more upright takeaway. Notice the line drawn from the butt of the club is pointing inside of my foot line as the club goes back. As it gets to the same position you see on the facing page, the club will be on a more vertical swing plane instead of the up-and-around fairway bunker arc. This is perfect for shorter, softer shots, but bad for playing out of fairway bunkers. You don't want to explode the ball; you want to *pick* it (page 44), taking very little sand.

**EXPLOSION OUT OF THE SAND**

# ADDRESS

Earlier, I mentioned that my fairway bunker swing is the same as my full swing. But, like everything else in golf, adjustments and modifications are occasionally required.

The main difference is the base you're standing on. Sand is not as firm as the ground, and if your lower body becomes too active during the swing, you slide out of position.

Maintaining a steady head throughout my swing makes it possible to return the clubhead to the same exact point. Check this head line in the rest of my swing positions.

Just as in my full swing, I want to establish a triangle with my shoulders, arms, hands and the grip of the club. The success of any full swing is keeping the butt of the club in front of the chest throughout the swing.

This is the position I want to return to at impact as I clip the ball off the sand. Notice that my right shoulder is lower than my left.

If your head sways or moves, chances are you'll hit the shot fat or thin, and neither result will help you master this trouble shot.

A good way to limit your lower body movement for fairway bunker shots is to pinch your feet and knees a little to the inside. This helps prevent left and right lower body movement.

I want to keep my weight almost equal on both feet, but a little more on my right foot at impact.

# TAKEAWAY

Swinging more with the upper half of your body is better for producing distance on fairway bunker shots. As you analyze this swing position, pay particular attention to the steady head and the angle forming in my right wrist.

My chin still points to the same position as it did at address. Your head is the centerpoint of your swing. Maintaining a steady head allows the clubhead to return to the exact point it left from—the back of your ball.

Good ballstrikers maintain this triangular relationship throughout their swing. The swing relies heavily on timing. Linking the chest, shoulders, arms, hands and grip produces consistent results. The butt of the club is still in front of my chest.

Notice how my right wrist has angled on the takeaway. I want to retain that wrist angle through impact to ensure a powerful exit from the bunker.

The key to a quiet lower body is not to move it left or right during the swing. Keeping the knees slightly pinched helps restrict its movement.

# PRE-IMPACT

Visualize the club continuing on past this position and picking the ball out of the bunker. As the club follows the powerful swing arc back to the ball, I will return to the same position that I began with at address.

You can play a variety of clubs out of fairway bunkers, including woods, as I'll show you next. The key is how much space you have to work with before the bunker lip comes into play.

Notice I've retained the angle set on my backswing. This is the angle you want for all phases of your long game. Never flip your wrists through a shot; power through them instead.

My weight is still distributed equally, with just a little more shifting to the right foot as I approach impact.

The swing arc shows that the clubhead will be sweeping through the ball instead of approaching from a steep angle. Like all correct power-producing shots, the clubhead is approaching the ball from the inside.

# IMPACT

In the normal golf swing, you get behind the ball and move ahead and hit it. But, especially with long fairway bunker play, the idea is to return to the same place you started.

This is more important than playing a shot off the fairway. If you hit it fat off the fairway, you can still get some distance. But hit it fat in the bunker and your ball will not go anywhere.

My head remained steady, with my chin still pointing to the same position it was at address. As a result, the lowest point of my swing arc did not move and the ball was picked cleanly off the sand.

The triangle, comprised of my chest, shoulders, arms, hands and the butt of the club, has returned to the address position here at impact.

### FOLLOW-THROUGH

*A good sign that you picked the ball off the sand is your ability to finish in an up-and-around follow-through position.*

# PLAYING A WOOD FROM A FAIRWAY BUNKER

You can easily hit a wood out of a fairway bunker, but the ground needs to be a little firmer. As for which wood to hit, do not attempt to use a 3-wood. A better choice would be a 4-wood or a 5-wood.

Another important aspect that must factor into your decision is the bunker's construction. Does it have a high lip? If the answer is yes, go with an iron instead. The lower wood launch angle makes it difficult to clear some fairway bunker lips.

Here are some tips from David Frost to help you decide which club to use and how to play a wood out of a fairway bunker.

## MATCH THE CLUB TO THE BUNKER

These two examples will help you determine which club to hit out of these fairway bunkers. Remember the two ingredients in the fairway bunker equation: **Escape plus distance.** You must escape before the ball can go anywhere!

*CHOOSE AN IRON*

*Should your ball end up this close to the lip, put the wood back in your bag. You need an iron to clear the lip. It's far better to sacrifice a little distance than to hit the bunker's face as a result of a wood's lower launch angle.*

*CHOOSE A WOOD*

*Balls this far away from the lip offer a much higher percentage of success playing your wood. I'll show you some tips on how to play the shot, but remember to use only a 4-wood or 5-wood.*

## FEEL THE SAND, POSITION YOUR HEAD

*Whichever club you take, learn to feel the sand when you get into the bunker. First, feel how much you can slide. Deep sand is a warning—guard against moving or sliding during your swing. Shallow sand, which is firmer, allows you to become more aggressive.*

*When you play a wood, feel like your head position stays behind the ball and never gets ahead of it. Check my head position through all the action photos on the coming pages. It does not move.*

# TEMPO AND TIMING

With a wood you have plenty of club in your hands to get the job done, so relax. You can ease up on your swing and not rush it. The swing key is to make a complete backswing and a complete follow-through. Think of it in these terms:

• Backswing: Back faces the target.

• Follow-through: Chest faces the target.

• Remember: Pinch your knees inward. This will restrict unwanted lower body movement.

*BACKSWING: BACK FACES TARGET*

*FOLLOW-THROUGH: CHEST FACES TARGET*

*Tempo and timing are critical when using a wood to "pick" your way out of a fairway bunker. Don't force things—you have plenty of power already, with that wood in your hands. Swing back and follow through completely and easily, with your back and then your chest facing the target.*

# TROUBLE SHOT:
# AVOIDING FAIRWAY BUNKER LIPS

With your ball close to the lip, a trouble shot that gets the ball up and out quickly while still eating up some of the distance to the pin is the solution. On page 55 you will see the result of playing this shot correctly. The ball quickly climbs over the lip and is free to fly down the fairway.

You need a checklist for success on this shot:

✔ Decide how to get the ball over the lip.

✔ Take enough club.

✔ Alter your stance to conform to the angle of the slope.

✔ Rehearse the shot.

✔ Hips, shoulders and head will lean back, restricting your backswing but creating more room for your distance-producing follow-through. This helps the ball both go up and travel down the fairway!

*REHEARSE*

*Take your stance and rehearse the shot. Develop a feeling for the angle it will take to clear the lip. Then select a club that will get the job done. Always develop confidence in your trouble shots before committing to them.*

## SET THE CORRECT ANGLE

Setting a correct angle to the slope allows a complete follow-through after impact. Shoulders, hips and knees all need to be set to the slope angle.

*SHOULDERS PARALLEL TO THE SLOPE*

*HIPS PARALLEL TO THE SLOPE*

*KNEES PARALLEL TO THE SLOPE*

*AVOID THIS POSITION*

*Leaning forward, thinking you are better balanced, is the wrong approach. Your backswing will be bigger, but the problem occurs when the club returns to the ball. This position encourages an incorrect chopping motion, which is not conducive to achieving distance. Remember the fairway bunker trouble shot equation: escape plus distance.*

laying a shot successfully near the bunker lip, as I have in the large photo on this page, is a result of setting up for the shot correctly and then applying the correct swing for the situation.

Just as we have in most of these fairway bunker shots, taking the club back inside the line on the backswing creates a longer swing arc for the distance you need to cover. Couple this with a complete follow-through and those close-to-the-lip bunker shots will no longer trouble you.

### BACKSWING

*Take the club back inside the line. Leaning back with your head, shoulders and hips will shorten your backswing but free up room for the swing-through.*

### FOLLOW-THROUGH

*Properly setting up at address allows me to follow through completely. I need to cover a lot of distance and a full follow-through helps.*

If you set the correct angle (shoulders, hips and knees parallel to the slope) you should be able to clear the bunker's lip with ease and still have enough power to get the ball down the fairway some distance.

# TROUBLE SHOT:
# BALL IN BUNKER/ STANCE ON GRASS

Your ball trickled into a bunker and now you're faced with two different substances to work with—grass and sand. But the real trouble in this shot is neither of those!

The ball is below your feet, and that's the situation you need to adjust to when faced with this fairway bunker problem. David Frost's solution is far simpler than you might think. How would you play the shot? If your answer is to bring your shoulders down to the ball, you're right … *if* the plan is carried out correctly.

## THE WRONG WAY AND THE RIGHT WAY

Bending over (left, below) is the incorrect way to bring your shoulders down to the ball. I simply widen my stance (right, below), which automatically lowers my shoulders closer to the ball. As you can see on page 57, I'm able to maintain my balance throughout the swing. I've never met a golfer who can consistently hit good shots from unbalanced positions.

*WRONG: DON'T BEND OVER*

*Bending over will hurt your balance.*

*RIGHT: WIDEN YOUR STANCE*

*Widening your stance will bring your shoulders closer to the ball and help you keep your balance.*

# SOLUTION: WIDEN YOUR STANCE

Golfers get themselves into trouble whenever excessive body movement creeps into their swings—and in this trouble shot it would be even deadlier. Widening my stance lowers my shoulders, which brings me closer to the ball and keeps me on a solid, balanced foundation; this discourages up or down motion.

As you can see in this combined-action swing photo, the images remain almost as one. To strike the ball well, you must return to an impact position that was similar to your address position. Unnecessary movement makes this difficult without compensations. Once a swing is underway, compensations never lead to consistent shotmaking! Structure your changes into your address positions instead.

Lowering your shoulders works in this trouble situation, but I also suggest one other slight adjustment—move slightly closer to the ball.

# TROUBLE SHOT:
# BALL ON GRASS/STANCE IN BUNKER

This is the opposite of our last trouble shot. Now the ball is above where you normally play it. In this case, eliminate some of the lean from your normal address position. Successfully playing this trouble shot requires:

- A more upright swing plane.

- Bringing your shoulders back, which makes you feel a little farther away from the ball but allows your hands to react through the impact position.

- Standing a little closer.

---

*ADJUST YOUR POSTURE*

*Bring your shoulders back.*

*UPRIGHT SWING PLANE*

*Bring your shoulders back naturally to create a more upright swing plane, which is needed to successfully play this trouble shot.*

## DAVID'S SHOTMAKING TIP

Bringing your shoulders back will set your swing up for a more upright swing plane. One other tip is your footing, since you are standing on the sand.

It's very important that you feel the sand as much as you feel the swing. Try to make yourself feel as if you're embedded in the sand, providing the stability for your shot.

# TROUBLE SHOT:
# STANCE ON GRASS AND SAND

Weighting is the key to mastering this trouble shot. How much you adjust your weight depends on how far you need to hit the ball. Since this is a long shot, requiring a 5- or 6-iron, I suggest feeling more weight on your right side so your club can do more of the work.

- More weight on the right side keeps your body away from the impact zone and creates a greater chance of swinging through correctly.

- The more weight you place on your left side, the more your body will get in the way.

---

### BACKSWING

*You can clearly see my body is staying behind the ball on my backswing. I feel the weight on the right side as a result.*

*Make some practice swings prior to addressing your ball (1).*

*Establish the feeling that your weight is on the right side of your body (2).*

### SWING THE CLUB THROUGH

*The club must be able to swing aggressively through the impact zone to create the needed power that propels the ball a long distance.*

*The club should be able to pass your body (1). Keep more weight on the right side of your body (2), so you can completely swing through.*

*If your body is ahead of the club due to weighting on your left side, the club will stay behind you all the time and you won't be able to swing through the shot.*

# FRANK'S TREE SAVES

On many courses, missing the fairway with your drive brings the trees into play. On the next few pages, Frank Lickliter shows you how to turn that trouble into opportunity instead.

We begin by determining the type of shot to play when facing this situation. Frank has chosen to fly over the tree, as you can see on these two pages. But on the following pages, he demonstrates other strategies and techniques to fly the ball under the branches or arc your ball's flight around the tree. Frank is using the same club for all of these shots, but you should always choose a club suitable to the task at hand. The technique takes care of the various ball flights.

## TROUBLE SHOT: OVER TREES

When you want your ball to fly over a tree on a high trajectory, just a few adjustments will help you play the shot consistently. Let's begin with ball positioning and the role of the shoulders.

### BALL FORWARD FOR HEIGHT

*The crossed clubs indicate my normal ball position. Notice I place the ball farther forward in my stance. Moving it up increases clubhead loft and makes it easy to keep my shoulders behind it.*

### SHOULDERS BEHIND BALL

*As you make your turn away, you want to feel your shoulders moving behind the ball. The dotted line shows my shoulders are behind the ball at the top of my backswing. Notice that my weight is still in the middle of my stance.*

# SOLUTION: HIGH LAUNCH ANGLE

The key to this shot is turning behind the ball and then staying behind it for the entire shot. Your spine is tilted back toward the right foot as you rotate with your shoulders. It all combines to produce a high launch angle, which will give you a fighting chance to get over that tree.

### SHOULDER ANGLE

*My spine is tilted toward my right foot. I want to feel that I can turn my shoulder over my right knee, which provides even more of an angle for the spine.*

### IMPACT

*I'm clearly staying behind the ball at impact. The spine is still tilted toward my right foot.*

The ball is launching at quite a steep angle—exactly what you want and need, to fly over a tree. Position the ball forward on your stance, then get your shoulders behind it.

### FOLLOW-THROUGH

*Keep turning with your shoulders all the way as you follow through.*

Mid-Course Corrections

# TROUBLE SHOT:
# GOING UNDER TREES

Another tree trouble shot option is hitting the ball under branches. A lower trajectory is needed for this knockdown trouble shot. Make sure you knock the trajectory down so a limb doesn't knock the ball down.

## BALL AND SHOULDER POSITIONS

*The farther-back ball position closes down the club, lessening loft. I don't choke down on the club.*

*Notice my shoulders are now ahead of the ball instead of behind it, as they were for the "over the tree" shot.*

*Finally, do not turn back as far as you would for a normal shot.*

## BEAT DOWN

*Going under a tree calls for an aggressive shot.*

*Notice my downswing looks as if I'm about ready to beat down on the ball.*

*Also notice that my torso is ahead of the ball.*

# SOLUTION: VISUALIZE TRAJECTORY

The intent of my swing adjustments is to launch the ball at a lower angle than normal, but with enough power to have it fly under the tree with a flatter trajectory. It should land off the green and then roll up the rest of the way. The large photo on this page shows that I've launched the ball aggressively and it will pass under the branches with plenty of clearance. Visualizing the trajectory programs your mind prior to hitting the shot.

### FINISH DOWN

*By setting up with the ball back in the stance your weight is going to be forward of the ball. The lower you want the shot, the more weight you shift to your left side. Keep your finish down as you come through the ball. Compare my follow-through photo with the one for the high flyer (page 61 lower right), and you'll see how different the two positions look. One created height, the other a lower, knockdown shot.*

# TROUBLE SHOT:
# DRAW AROUND THE TREES

Even though you would not play a draw around the tree in the previous examples, these two pages will demonstrate the technique changes you'll need when the opportunity arises. You're probably as likely to need a draw as a fade, as far as tree troubles are concerned.

Draw the ball using your shoulders. Make a pretty normal swing except close the clubface slightly at address and then make your left shoulder go up.

*SETUP*

*I closed my clubface slightly and set up my body more parallel to the target line. Remember it was open for the fade. My ball position is slightly forward.*

*SHOULDER PROMOTES DRAW*

*I want to feel my left shoulder moving up as the downswing begins (1). This will drop the clubhead to more of an inside swing plane (2), promoting a draw.*

**1**

The clubhead came from inside the target line and has returned to the inside again following impact. I'm rotating the right forearm over the left, closing the clubface. A hook spin was applied to the ball and it will fly around the tree before bending back to land on the green.

**2**

## FRANK'S SHOTMAKING TIP

Practice flying the ball differently on the range so that when trouble comes your way you can aim straight at it, change your ball position and stance and fly over, under, left or right of the trouble.

Begin by slightly changing your ball position and finish by rotating the right forearm over the left (1). Be sure to follow through completely (2) and finish the swing. These are clear signs the ball will fly on a draw trajectory. While the techniques are different, it will be very easy for you to remember the simple changes I made for each ball flight.

Mid-
Course
Corrections

You can use ball position and your finish to shape a shot around trouble. Frank Lickliter is exactly correct when he demonstrates playing the ball back for fades and forward for draws. Perhaps you learned it differently. I'll show you why Frank is right.

## BALL POSITION DRILL

As you swing, the clubface is rotating except for the fraction of a second when it squares to the target line at impact. To prove the point, tee up three balls (as I have below) along your inside/square/inside swing arc and place a shaft at your normal ball position for reference.

*Tee up three balls like this to start the drill.*

### *OPEN CLUBFACE = FADE*

*If you hit the ball before you get to your normal ball position, as a result of playing it back in your stance, the face will be open and the ball will fade.*

### *SQUARE POSITION = STRAIGHT SHOT*

*If impact is at the bottom of your swing arc, the clubface will be square to the target line at impact and your shot will be straight.*

### *CLOSED CLUBFACE = DRAW*

*Impact past the normal ball position, as a result of playing it forward in your stance, closes the face and the ball will draw.*

# SHAPE YOUR FINISH

How you shape your finish is also important to whether you create a draw or fade. Practice by trying to shape your shots around your golf bag, as I'm doing in the two photos on this page.

• The lower the right shoulder and the straighter the shaft at the finish, the more likely you are to hit a fade.

• The higher the right shoulder and the flatter the shaft at the finish, the more likely you are to hit a draw.

*RIGHT SHOULDER LOW = FADE*

*RIGHT SHOULDER HIGH = DRAW*

*To fade the ball around my bag I tee the ball back in my stance and finish with my right shoulder low. Compare this shaft position to the one on the right.*

*To draw the ball around my bag I tee the ball up in my stance and finish with my right shoulder higher. Notice how flat the shaft is compared to the fade finish.*

## MARTIN'S FADE & DRAW CRIB NOTES

This simple summary should help you remember how to create fades and draws.

|        | Ball Position | Clubface at Impact | Finish Position     |
|--------|---------------|--------------------|---------------------|
| **Fade** | Back          | Open               | Right Shoulder Low  |
| **Draw** | Forward       | Closed             | Right Shoulder High |

# 4 TROUBLE SHOTS WITHIN 100 YARDS

*"Rehearse! You can do a couple things to promote the correct swing for any situation. I suggest rehearsing them before hitting the shot."—David Frost*

**W**ho's in charge, you or the ball? Before answering, read this chapter. The ball may have had a mind of its own by getting blocked behind the tree, but Ian Baker-Finch and Skip Kendall will soon have you back in control.

Fans marvel and cheer at the seemingly impossible shots PGA TOUR players conjure up (and make!) in crucial situations. But the bottom line is that the pros understand what makes a ball react in a certain way, then improvise a plan to fit the situation.

Is your backswing really blocked by a tree branch? Perhaps. Skip suggests a more angled backswing that steepens its arc to avoid tree trouble shots. For times when you're really blocked, his trouble shots teach you to handle problems on both the backswing and follow-through. He even plays a shot left-handed with an upside-down sand wedge to escape trouble!

Ian leads off with a short lesson on making the ball fly high or low. After all, these guys are more than just good. They're in control.

*"What's over there, a nudist colony?"—Lee Trevino (after three playing partners all hit their drives strong but into the woods.)*

# TROUBLE SKILLS:
# IAN'S BALL FLIGHT FORMULA

The tree in front of Ian's ball will help you earn your flight wings. On these two pages, you'll learn a simple formula for high- or low-flying approach shots to the green. Think of it this way:

- High Shot = Hands High
- Low Shot = Hands Low

Your follow-through position should look like one of the above equations when the ball starts behaving as you wish. But, as with all trouble shot techniques and improvisations, first you must decide on the strategy to match your situation. In these two cases, let's limit your choices to either flying over or under a tree that's immediately blocking your scoring zone path to the hole.

*PLANNING THE SHOT*

*Up and over, with a soft landing, is the right plan for this ball.*

## HIGH FLYER

High-flying shots offer the ability to make a soft landing on the green. As with all golf shots, the address position sets the stage for the proper execution. Look closely at mine.

*BALL FORWARD*

*When you want the ball to fly high and land soft, stay behind the shot. Using a wedge, I position the ball forward in my stance.*

*The forward ball position makes staying behind it during the swing an easy proposition. Even just past impact, as the ball is headed up, I stay back.*

# LOW FLYER

Low flying shots are usually played when you are so close to an obstruction that enough distance is not available to allow for a high trajectory. So the choice switches to a low flying ball that must land short of the green and roll up. Always look at the potential landing areas ahead, using the contours as an advantage. Land the ball on the target and allow the contours to feed the ball to the green.

*You'll have to hit this shot low, letting the ball hit ahead of the green and roll the rest of the way there.*

### HIGH FOLLOW-THROUGH

*The old reversed "C" is the perfect swing thought for a high flying fol-low-through. Notice my hands finish above my shoulders.*

### IMPACT

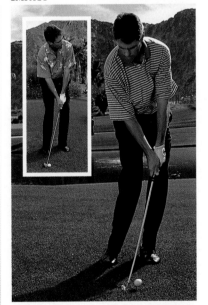

*Impact mirrors my address position (inset). The ball was played back in my stance. My hands stay ahead of the clubhead through impact. This is a punch shot, but it's not a quick, jerky motion. I always maintain my same swing tempo and timing for every shot.*

### LOW FOLLOW-THROUGH

*With a punch shot, you are not trying to stop the club at the ball; it just appears that way. Because the hands are advancing in front of the clubhead, they finish low. The clubhead finishes low and, most important, the ball tracks low.*

Trouble
Shots
Within
100 Yards

73

# TROUBLE SHOT:
# HOOK SPIN UNDER TREE

During the third round of the 2001 Bay Hill Invitational, Skip Kendall hit a perfect tee shot only to find it here after it took a bad bounce off a fairway downslope. The only shot he could play is the one we deal with on these two pages: a hook spin, under and around the tree, that can run up to the green.

### CLOSE THE CLUBFACE

*If you have to hit to the right of a tree trunk, the hook shot is already set up, because you must aim the ball to the right anyway. Closing the clubface so it's almost in line with the target, but still aiming your body right, promotes an easy way to execute a hook.*

### ADDRESS

*Just the path of the club will make the ball hook, if you close the face while aligning your body position to the right of your target. Play the ball slightly back in your stance.*

### LEVEL SWING

*To keep the hook low, your shoulders must remain level during the swing. Make a few practice swings, like a baseball player rehearsing level shoulder rotation.*

# SOLUTION: THE GREAT ESCAPE!

The ball is curving around the tree on its way to Bay Hill's 15th green. Arnold Palmer planted these magnolia trees as a tribute to Augusta National. Land between them and your only choice is playing a shot like this.

### BACKSWING

Notice I've slightly choked down on the club. Smooth swings lead to solid contact at impact—vital if you want to start shaping shots. A shorter swing works best if you have fairway to go through. But if you have to roll the ball through the rough, hit it a little harder.

### IMPACT

The ball starts right of the tree and will hook from right to left back toward the target. Just as Ian demonstrated for low shots, I finish low. A hook roll stays low to the ground but has the energy to roll a long distance after landing.

# TROUBLE SHOT:
# LOW RUNNING FADE

Compounding the problem for playing these shots is that you are almost always in the rough, unless, of course, you're behind the fairway tree on the 18th hole at Pebble Beach.

Playing a low running fade is almost opposite to playing a low running hook, although they share one similarity—the need for a level swing. Should the shoulders dip at any time, the ball flight goes up and gets knocked down quickly by a branch.

*OPEN THE FACE*

*The low running fade setup features my body aimed to the left, but the clubface is opened and pointing toward the target. A natural swing along my bodyline fades the ball around the tree. Ball position in the middle of my stance keeps it low.*

*IMPACT*

*Good contact is vital for working the ball in specific directions. Partial contact can't place the correct spin on the ball. Don't rush your swing because of the trouble!*

# SOLUTION: FADING TOWARD HOME

The ball is fading nicely around the tree and will move low and to the right. With bunkers around the green, you may prefer to stop the shot a little short of the green, at least until reading David Frost's greenside bunker tips in Chapter 6.

## BACKSWING

*A slightly choked down grip is visible, and so are my level shoulders. Practice the level baseball swing to program yourself for this swing.*

## SLICE SPIN

*This is one of those times when applying slice spin is okay. Notice the open club-face is approaching the ball from outside the target line. A left-to-right spin is applied to the ball at impact, so it starts out left and slices low to the right.*

# TROUBLE SHOT:
# BLOCKED BACKSWING

In this case, the tree is definitely blocking Skip's backswing, but all is not lost. Realistically advancing the ball to the green is out of the equation, so be smart about your remaining options. Look at every option, including getting down on your knees to hit the shot.

Decide how far you need to advance the ball to a spot where you can get up and down. If you feel comfortable hitting into the green with a 60-yard wedge, play to that spot, instead of trying to reach a spot 30 yards from the green. Play to your strengths.

*REHEARSE YOUR SHOT*

*Ease your anxiety by rehearsing and feeling how far you can go back, making sure you have enough club to get the distance you need. Rehearsing this a number of times, and feeling the club accelerate down and through the impact area, builds confidence and allows you to stay in control. Your backswing needs to be as close to the tree as possible. Choke down for more control.*

# SOLUTION: UN-BLOCKED FOLLOW-THROUGH

The tree interferes with your backswing, but not your follow-through. Accelerate as much as you can through the shot to reach your target distance. Think of this trouble shot as a big chip shot.

### BIG CHIP SHOT

*The similarities between this blocked backswing trouble shot and a chip shot can be seen in both photos. The club swings back a limited and controlled distance (1) and comes through impact with the hands leading (2). Accelerate through the shot, but stay in control and finish higher than for a normal chip.*

# TROUBLE SHOT:
# BLOCKED FOLLOW-THROUGH

When an obstruction, like this tree, blocks your follow-through, the first step is assessing the danger to your physical well- being. Play a normal shot as long as the tree can't hurt you. These are only branches, but if a solid tree trunk were the problem, another type of shot should be your choice to avoid injury.

You can hit the branches on your follow-through and cause leaves to fall, without incurring a penalty stroke, because you hit the ball. Knocking leaves down with a practice swing is a possible penalty situation.

*If you hit the ball and knock a few leaves down on your follow-through, there's no penalty. But don't knock leaves down with a practice swing—that could cost you a penalty stroke because you've improved your situation.*

*Take an extra club (5-iron instead of a 6-iron) and choke down (inset). Relax and feel tension-free to stay in control. Successful shots must have rhythm and freedom. Tension tightens muscles and creates jerky swings.*

*Impact is normal after a backswing that is made tension-free and under control. Danger lies ahead, but it's not apparent in this close-up position of my lower body as the club launches the ball. My concentration was on the stroke, not the tree.*

**BALL ON TARGET**

*I'm just making a normal swing, even though I know the shaft will soon hit the branches. Small branches are no problem; see pages 84-85 for what to do when tree trunks get in your way.*

**BRANCH CONTACT**

*The club does get absorbed in the branches, but my concentration on making a normal swing allowed the ball to advance down the fairway. This is a par-5 hole, so my swing was geared to a layup shot rather than trying to reach the green over water.*

## SKIP'S STRATEGY

Even as you master these trouble shots, always be realistic about your chances. Controlling ball flight is even more beneficial once you learn to reach the distances that work best for your scoring opportunities.

Trouble
Shots
Within
100 Yards

# TROUBLE SHOT:
# REVERSE SIDES

*The only solution to a lie like this: reverse sides.*

If your ball lands in this situation (top left photo), check your health policy and make sure the premiums are paid before trying to play a normal shot. This is one risk/reward scenario where the risk factor far outweighs the reward.

Have you ever wanted to play a shot from the opposite side? Right-handers, this is your moment to be Phil Mickelson, as Skip Kendall demonstrates his reverse side shot.

### PLAY LEFT-HANDED WITH AN UPSIDE-DOWN WEDGE

### ADJUSTMENTS

*My glove goes into my pocket, because it's going to be a left-handed shot. My trusty sand wedge is the club of choice.*

*I practice this shot occasionally, just in case it's needed. That's why my left-handed setup looks so natural. I have a neutral grip with the V's pointed at my chest. Have you noticed the one major difference? I've turned the wedge upside down (inset), pointing the toe to the ground.*

*Staying in control, my swing looks pretty good at both the top of my backswing (1) and as I'm closing in on the ball (2). Switching to a left-handed approach to this shot was my only option for advancing the ball back in position in the fairway.*

*OK, so I'm not Phil Mickelson, but the solid impact on the upside-down clubface (inset) shows the results are pretty good for a part-time lefty. The fans would applaud my improvisational skills, but I have practiced this shot many times before.*

Trouble
Shots
Within
100 Yards

# TROUBLE SHOT:
# CONTROLLING AN UPHILL WEDGE

The trend in modern golf course architecture features a lot of mounding around greens. Sometimes missing the green with an approach shot puts you on a severe upward or downward slope.

You're in the scoring zone, but this trouble shot affects the normal distance you would hit a club, because the slope sends the ball higher and shorter. Losing your balance and improper weighting contribute to the problem.

*Uphill lies require some pre-shot adjustments.*

### LESS LOFTED CLUB

*You will hit the ball a lot higher, so if you want to control your distance, compensate by taking a less lofted club. In this case, I'm switching from a pitching wedge to an 8-iron.*

### SET UP TO THE SLOPE

*All through this book, you will see the four of us pose in this position. It's important. Setting your body to the slope allows you to remain in balance throughout the swing. Widening your stance enhances your stability.*

# SOLUTION: REDUCE THE HEIGHT

The correct way to play this trouble shot is to make an easy-flowing swing with plenty of club. You don't want to swing too hard. As you swing through the ball, try to get forward in your follow-through so your weight is on your left side. It's important to hold your finish.

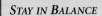

*STAY IN BALANCE*

*Notice my swing has balance and rhythm, both when I'm at the top of my backswing (1) and finishing my follow-through (2). I'm not trying to hit the ball higher. My thought is to feel the distance I need and swing accordingly, staying in balance and holding my finish on the left side. I use my right foot as a brace.*

# TROUBLE SHOT:
# CONTROLLING A DOWNHILL WEDGE

The first step in playing either an uphill or (in this case) a downhill wedge is club selection. Skip switched from a wedge to an 8-iron for the uphill shot, since he wanted a less lofted club to control the height and distance.

For downhill shots, you want a club with as much loft as possible to help get the ball in the air. Stay in control. This shot is difficult enough without bellying the ball and sending it racing uncontrollably along the ground. We're in the scoring zone: Precision is vital, even in trouble situations.

*When preparing for a downhill wedge shot, use a club with more loft than you usually would select for that distance.*

### ALIGN TO THE SLOPE

*Set your body angles to the slope. You must swing along the slope line to get the ball airborne from a lie that fights it all the way.*

### TAKE TWO CLUBS

*We play with caddies, so our clubs are always with us. If you're sharing a cart or the ball is in a spot carts can't go to, always bring a couple or three clubs along. Never force the wrong club to make the correct shot. The odds are against it. The best way to avoid additional trouble is to understand the technique and have the correct club to get yourself back in position, on the fairway or green.*

# SOLUTION: CREATE A HIGHER TRAJECTORY

Your lie increases in difficulty if you're playing the wedge out of the rough. It's really a guessing game as to hitting it fat or catching a flyer. Here are the keys to success:

• Set your body to the slope.

• Make a full, flowing swing.

• Stay in balance so you don't end up running down the slope after hitting the shot.

## STAY IN CONTROL

*Making a controlled, easy swing allows me to maintain my balance all through the shot. The slope de-lofts the club, which is the reason for selecting a club with more loft.*

One thing to remember is that the ball will fly lower than a normal wedge. This means it will run after landing instead of sticking. Choose a target that takes this into consideration. Aim for the front of the green for back pins and the apron for close pins.

# PRACTICE TEE

You do not have to go onto the course to practice your trouble shots. Many of them can be easily practiced on the range using your golf bag to simulate the trunk of a tree. Or stick an old shaft in the ground at an angle to simulate low-hanging branches.

If your friends question if you've gone totally mad, they'll quickly change their tune when they see you hit shots backward or at angles to your bag. Watching you extricate yourself from seemingly impossible trouble will probably send them to the practice range too!

## REVERSE SHOT

An alternative to Skip Kendall's reverse shot is to hit a blocked ball backward instead of from the opposite side. As you can see, my normal right-handed stance is blocked by my bag (my simulated tree trunk for practice purposes). Here's how to practice playing the shot.

### 2- PICK UP THE CLUB

*Pick the club straight up with a wrist-cocking motion.*

### 1- REVERSE SETUP

*These two views clearly show how to set up for the backward shot. The ball should be positioned well in front of you to play the shot since you will be making a sharply descending attack angle (1). Choke down on the grip to shorten the club (2) and align the clubface with a target line that will get you back into the fairway and away from additional trouble.*

### 3- IMPACT

*Bring the club straight down to impact the ball and send it running on a line that returns you to the fairway or at least away from additional trouble.*

## BLOCKED BACKSWING

My bag could be a tree stump, a stake or even a boulder for this practice drill. No matter. My backswing is restricted. I can either take a one-stroke penalty and get relief from an unplayable lie … or use a technique to clear a backswing path.

The choice is yours depending on the shot. Be sure to factor in any other trouble you would face even with taking relief, including the distance remaining.

### 1- ALIGN CLUBFACE

### 2- CHANGE BODY POSITION

*Align your clubface to your target line, which in this case may just be an escape route back to the fairway away from all trouble.*

*I've adjusted my body so my back is facing the target as the clubhead still stays on line. This will not be a backward shot and I'll be able to make a backswing between my body and the bag.*

### SLOTTED SWING

*The backswing goes back in the slot between the bag and my body (1). The key here is that the clubface was aligned to an escape route target line and when it squares back to the ball at impact (2) it will send it on that line. Timing and tempo are important, so do not rush the shot. But before you shoot, make several practice strokes to program your mind and body for this different type of swing.*

## ON YOUR KNEES

If you are going to hit the ball while on your knees—I am using the shaft to simulate a low tree branch—would you choose a lofted iron or a driver? You don't really want to use a lofted iron. The heel will hit the ground and turn the club, resulting in a shot that goes off to the left. I suggest using a driver and develop the feeling of hitting down on it.

One more word of caution: Do not place a towel under your knees, as Craig Stadler did during a tournament in San Diego. A viewer saw the tape and phoned in that Craig had purposely improved his lie, which he innocently did. Put on your rain-suit pants if you don't want to get dirty.

### SETUP

*Choke down slightly and address the ball on the heel of the driver (inset).*

### BACKSWING

*Notice I am making a good-sized backswing. The swing arc will be level and produce a low running shot. If you need to carry trouble with a high flyer, you might be better served by taking a one-shot penalty and dropping the ball, according to The Rules of Golf for "no nearer the hole" relief.*

### GOOD CONTACT

*This action shot proved I hit it off my knees and the ball is off and running. Practice this shot on the range and use an old shaft to simulate a low branch, as I have.*

Trouble
Shots
Within
100 Yards

# 5 TROUBLE AROUND THE GREEN

*"You have to accept trouble shots. Turn that potential double bogey into a bogey or even a par. Just remember not to bite off more than you can chew."*
—Ian Baker-Finch

Your ball missed the green and now, with the pin so close, you are facing another trouble shot. Perhaps your ball is on a steep downward slope behind the green, or needs to be threaded between two trees. It could be up against the collar, where the rough meets the fringe, or deep in the wiry stuff around the green.

Regardless of the trouble, the task at hand is to play a shot that ends up close to the hole.

In this chapter, Frank, Ian and Skip share strategies and demonstrate how to accomplish that.

You'll learn to play the shots, and also learn why some pros grind the bounce out of their sand wedge. That's why they look so flat on television.

When facing trouble shots during tournament play, our professionals analyze the problem, consider several options and then commit to the shot. Why they choose to play one trouble shot solution over another provides the basis for a thought process you can take to the course.

**"Still your shot are the three ugliest words in golf."**—Dave Marr

# TROUBLE SHOT:
# DOWNHILL PITCH FROM HEAVY ROUGH

**H**ere on the 16th hole of the TPC at Sawgrass, my ball missed the green and nestled in the long grass above it. We shot this two weeks before THE PLAYERS Championship, so you are seeing what we face during tournament week.

I need to play a shot that would get the ball out and close to the pin. When you are faced with this shot, always remember that the club needs an angle coming into the ball. But, first, here's how I initially set up for the shot.

### SELECT A LANDING TARGET

*Select a landing target on the line to the hole.*

*The target should be on the next cut of rough before the green, to help slow the ball.*

*Align yourself to that target.*

### OPEN THE CLUBFACE

**Normal Shot**   **Downhill Shot**

*The more downhill the shot, the more loft is taken off the club. Compensate by opening the club more than you would for a normal shot.*

# SOLUTION: PICK AN INTERIM TARGET

The large photo here shows that my ball finished close to the hole, because I was able to get it up and out of the tall grass and land it on an interim target. Selecting the pin as your target could send the ball over the green and, in this case, into the water. Some other checkpoints for success appear here.

### 1- SET UP TO THE SLOPE

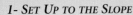

*Set your shoulders, hips and knees parallel to the slope you're on. The club needs angle coming into the ball, and if your shoulders are incorrectly level to the horizon, you can't create an angle.*

### 2- BACKSWING

*Your angled shoulders help create impact loft for a shot that fights it all the way. The key is to bring the club down to the ball without catching a lot of rough. A short, steep back-swing works best.*

### 3- IMPACT

*The ball pops out from the downward attack angle, coupled with the pre-set open clubface. You never know if you are going to get a flyer out of the rough, so remember to select an aiming target on the next cut of rough instead of shooting to the pin.*

# TROUBLE SHOT:
# SEVERE DOWNHILL LIE TO A CLOSE PIN

Y ou may want to think of this shot as "Ian's 60/60," since I'm going to use a 60-degree wedge and this slope is also about 60 degrees. The Tradition is a beautiful golf course with spectacular views, but, as you can see, this shot is tough.

The pin is near the edge of the green, and here I am perched on a very severe downslope trying to get it close. If you face this type of shot, anything on the green is a good result. To help, land the ball short of the green to scrub off some speed of the forward motion. I begin by adapting my stance to the terrain.

**SETUP**

*Choke down to the bottom of the grip with very light grip pressure.*

*Widen your stance for the stability needed to squarely impact the ball and finish in balance.*

*Your shoulders should be parallel to the downslope, and your weight is more on the lower leg to act as a brace.*

*I've slightly opened the face of my 60-degree wedge.*

**BACKSWING**

*You don't want to duff the ball or hit it fat in this situation. A partial backswing allows me to stay in balance to deliver the open clubface under the ball.*

# SOLUTION: BALANCE PLUS AN OPEN CLUBFACE

The wildflowers and mountain range in the background are beautiful, but the loft obtained from this tough lie is even more impressive. The key is staying in balance and continuing the clubhead parallel down the slope, ensuring the open face has the power to propel the ball higher into the air.

### STAY IN BALANCE

Notice how my clubface remains open and parallel to the slope as it passes the ball (1). That's a good sign, as the ball is going up instead of just forward. The height creates a softer landing with less roll.

In my balanced follow-through (2), the face is still open. From this lie, it will be hard to judge the distance. Pat yourself on the back if the ball finishes on the green.

# TROUBLE SHOT:
# HITTING BETWEEN OBSTACLES

When faced with this lie, your first course of action is to decide whether you can fly the ball over the trouble or must punch it through. A lot depends on your current level of play. You can be more aggressive the better skilled you are.

Here Ian Baker-Finch decides the lower punch shot is the best choice. He begins by selecting an interim spot three or four feet in front of the ball to fire over, just as Jack Nicklaus has done so successfully over the years. Once you are positive you are aiming the clubface where it will avoid the trouble, it takes a lot of apprehension out of the shot.

*FIRE OVER A CLOSE AIMING SPOT*

*I found a leaf a few feet in front of the ball and on the line to the hole. This makes it easy to align the club precisely in the direction I want the ball to take off between the trouble on both sides. If you are worried about where the clubhead is aimed, the anxiety will not allow your swing to be fluent.*

*Always take at least two clubs with you. Most duffed shots are either because of apprehension or lack of planning. I brought my 9-iron and 60-degree wedge, since I wasn't sure if the best shot would be over or through the trees.*

*To play a punch shot, I'm using my 9-iron. The ball is back in my stance and the shaft is angled forward to de-loft the club.*

*The punch shot is a good choice for this trouble shot because the ball will stay low, avoiding the trouble on both sides. It lands short of the green but has plenty of momentum to roll close to the hole. The low flight you see here was set up by how the ball was positioned at address.*

**BETWEEN THE TROUBLE**

*The ball is flying low between the trees as a result of:*

- *Correct ball position at address.*

- *Forward shaft angle.*

- *Close target to aim to.*

- *Normal swing tempo.*

## CONTROLLING BALL FLIGHT

- Ball back with a low finish = lower ball flight
- Ball forward with a higher finish = higher ball flight

Trouble
Around
the Green

# TROUBLE SHOT:
# STEEP FLY OVER

Flying the ball over this palm tree, which is on line to the hole, is a "10" in degree of difficulty. It's a do or die shot, where you may need to get up and down to win a match with your buddies. Normally, you could just chip a 9-iron to the side of the palm, leaving a long putt.

The shot I'll play, though, is a high lob, where the ball must climb rapidly with very little forward motion. This is what you see Phil Mickelson do, when he takes a full swing with his lob wedge.

**SETUP**

*I set up with a very stable base and feel my weight behind the ball. I need a very shallow swing path to get this ball high, so I open the face of my 60-degree wedge. Notice my shoulders are angled slightly upward.*

**BACKSWING**

*Such a full backswing for only a short shot? Exactly! The longer your swing, the higher the ball goes, but not necessarily longer.*

# SOLUTION: HIGH FLYER

This photo shows my ball is headed almost vertically up and over the tree. The open face, a correctly angled body and full swing makes this possible. You must commit to the shot, because if you ease up at all, the match is over. The more you open the face, the higher the ball goes and the quicker it will stop.

*IMPACT*

The clubhead has passed the ball. The open clubface and shallow swing arc converted the swing power into a vertical leap. The ball will go high and then arc slightly forward as it climbs over the tree.

*FOLLOW-THROUGH*

My follow-through shows my weight is more on my back leg. My shoulders are angled upward. I swung through the ball, allowing the pre-set angles and open clubface to take care of the height needed to clear the tree.

# TROUBLE SHOT:
# FLY OVER THE HAZARD

It's obvious that the one thing you don't want to do is land a shot like this from the rough, into the water. Without any land to work with, a running shot is out of the question. That means trouble, if you have problems flying over no-escape situations.

The first step (below) is showing you the cause of so many missed shots that cause penalty situations as the ball finds the water.

*THE PROBLEM: ACTIVE LOWER BODY*

*Too much lower body action is the cause of most problems. If this is your backswing, it's difficult to control where the club will end up as it starts down. If you dip down with your body or your head, you will hit a fat shot and splash!*

*THE FIX: QUIET LOWER BODY*

*Skilled players have quiet lower bodies to allow the club position to always be in front, regardless of the swing position. I'm referring to the grip, and it must be in front of the chest from address to follow-through.*

# SOLUTION: FOCUS ON CLEARING THE HAZARD

The ball is gaining altitude and will fly over the water, landing softly on the green. Avoid the mistake of making the pin your target. The green slopes down from the pin to the water. Short shots might roll back down the slope and splash!

Give yourself plenty of room for some margin of error. A putt back down the hill is preferable to having to drop your next ball in a penalty situation.

*My hips have cleared as the club is coming into contact with the ball. Throughout this entire stroke have you noticed how the club is in front of my body? Your entire game will improve once you put this into practice.*

### BACKSWING

*This shot only requires going back to the 9 o'clock position. Notice how quiet my lower body is at the top of my backswing. My hands and the butt of the club are in front of my chest, showing I'm in control.*

### FOLLOW-THROUGH

*Is the club in front of my body in this position? The butt of the club is. The common misunderstanding is thinking the club-head must be in front. That's only true in the impact zone.*

### DOWNSTROKE

*Notice how my lower body remains quiet on the down-stroke. My hands and the butt of the club are still in front of my chest.*

Trouble Around the Green

# TROUBLE SHOT:
# SNAGLY LIES

I still need to fly the shot over the water, but on some of the tournament courses we play the grass can be snagly. That's my word for deep and grabby. Here's my solution.

### 1- OPEN THE CLUBFACE

**1-Square**     **2-Open**

*The deep grass wants to grab your clubface and turn it over. I play the shot by adjusting my wedge from the square position (1) to a more open one (2). This allows the club-face to skid through the grass, lifting the ball up and out.*

### 2- 9 O'CLOCK BACKSWING

*With the same quiet lower body as on pages 102 and 103, swing the club back to the 9 o'clock position. This gives you plenty of control and power for playing this trouble shot.*

*With the ball slightly back in my stance, the open clubface slides through the grass and under the ball, popping it up and out of the snagly grass. Notice the clubhead path as it passes under the ball.*

*The ball quickly gains forward momentum and the needed height to fly over the water hazard. The reasons:*

- *The open clubface.*

- *A quiet lower body.*

- *Keeping the butt of the club and my hands in front of my chest throughout the swing.*

Trouble
Around
the Green

# TROUBLE SHOT:
# POP SHOT

Sometimes the collar of the second cut of rough stops your ball if it rolls through the green. How do you play a shot that requires the clubhead to pass through the taller grass before impacting a ball sitting on the fringe?

That really depends on the height of the grass. I'll show you two ways to play this shot, and Skip will demonstrate one with his driver in Chapter 7. In this case, if the grass is long, play the pop shot.

### BACKSWING

*The ball is played back in my stance, because I want the club to start back on a very steep angle. This way you pass up all the rough that's behind the ball.*

# SOLUTION: VISUALIZE THE SHOT, POP IT IN

I give a lot of thought to every trouble shot. Deciding on the best way to play, and then correctly executing the shot, saves you strokes. Before playing the shot, practice a few different options and see which one provides the best opportunity for success.

Program your mind by visualizing the shot you selected and see the ball go toward the hole. Then step in and play that shot like a pro. In this photo, I've successfully played this shot from against the fringe. More important, the ball is following the exact path I visualized.

**IMPACT**

*I let the club fall right back to the ball, as seen here at impact. With a downhill lie, I only have to bump it about two feet. Since the arms don't move from in front of the body, the follow-through is just as you see here.*

# TROUBLE SHOT:
# BELLY CHIP

Another solution when your ball is up against the collar is to strike the ball at its equator with your wedge. This is a reliable shot to play when the rough behind the ball is not too high.

Here's a special tip for success: Skimming the clubhead back and through along the top of the rough impacts the ball at its equator, or belly, every time. As you play the shot, have the feeling of a low and slow pendulum putting stroke.

*1- SKIM BACK*

*Use the top of the rough as a guide. Skim the clubhead away from the belly of the ball.*

*2- SKIM THROUGH*

*Skim the clubhead along the top of the rough toward the belly of the ball. Impact will be at the equator, and your belly chip will get the job done.*

# TROUBLE SHOT:
# PUTTING CHIP

You'll encounter this most difficult lie when your ball is in four to five inches of rough and the grain is growing into it. The grass wants to grab the club, so the solution is to offer up only a small portion of the clubface.

Play this shot by closing the face of your wedge and adjusting your stance so it addresses the ball with a closed face on the toe. To make the club more vertical, adapt your regular putting address.

### 1- ADDRESS

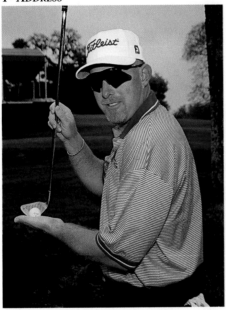

*This is how the club should be at address—vertical so it rests on the toe. Grip the wedge like your putter and close the face to the line about 30 degrees.*

### 2- BACKSWING

*Your backswing closely resembles your putting backstroke. Notice I'm using my putting grip.*

### 3- PRE-IMPACT

*The clubhead is returning to the ball and only the toe will impact the ball.*

### 4- IMPACT

*Where a regular chip might get caught up in the grass, the putting chip comes out on line every time. With the face closed and the wedge on its toe, the clubface slides easily through the grass.*

Trouble
Around
the Green

# TROUBLE SHOT:
# LOOSE LIES

The way you play this shot is determined by the lie. With your ball in pine needles, mulch or whatever else the superintendent uses on your course, you need to play a shot that slips under the ball, negating the looseness of the lie.

Use a little more hand action and keep your arms quiet. Your hands will open the clubface on the backswing and bottom it out on the return under the ball. The key to this is relaxing your grip to free up your hands.

### LOOSE LIE

*Be very careful about grounding your club when the lie is loose like this one. Hover the club instead of grounding it. PGA TOUR rules official Mark Russell explains more about this in Chapter 8.*

### HAND ACTION

*My arms are staying still as the hands take the club back, opening the clubface. Relax your grip to free up your hands.*

# SOLUTION: SLOW DOWN FOR SUCCESS

When I'm asked about why a pro's hand/eye coordination seems to be better than most amateur players', my answer is simple: We do things slowly, while amateurs do them fast. There is no need to be impatient or quick with this swing. The key to playing this trouble shot successfully is being slow and smooth. If you do that, all your loose lie shots will look like mine here.

### BACKSWING

*Just a partial backswing is all you need for this shot. This changes somewhat, depending on the distance to the green.*

### PRE-IMPACT

*A relaxed grip is allowing my hands to slip the clubface under the ball, negating the loose lie. Notice how level the clubface is while approaching the ball.*

# TROUBLE SHOT:
# HARDPAN LIES

Depending on where you play, you'll encounter various tight lies. It could be dry, hard, almost shiny dirt or it's Southern cousin clay. No matter what the substrate though, the lie makes it difficult to get the leading edge of the club to the ball.

The problem may not always be with your technique; it may be the bounce of your club. Here is a true TOUR pro secret. Let's look at how some of the players on TOUR customize their sand wedges, and then make this shot with the fine-tuned club.

## REMOVE THE BOUNCE

Bounce is the portion of your sand wedge that extends below the leading edge. It's the flange on the back of the club. I've ground about 4 to 10 grams of steel off this area (1). In a sense, I've taken the bounce out of my sand wedge.

I can hit a nice high flop shot off of a hardpan lie. Even laying the club flat down on bare ground (2) shows the leading edge is touching it, allowing me to easily get the club under the ball. Most amateurs have a gap between the ground and the edge. Now you know our secret!

### 1- ADDRESS

*To start to make the shot, open your stance a little and position the shaft slightly forward. This creates the angle that keeps the clubface's leading edge on the ground.*

### 2- BACKSWING

*This is more of a putting stroke, with very little hand action. Just take it back slowly, allowing it to open slightly.*

*Pros do things slowly, and you want solid contact but not a lot of speed at impact. Be sure to follow through low to the ground.*

*Hardpan shots are no longer trouble when you use Frank's tips for playing the shot.*

Trouble
Around
the Green

# PRACTICE TEE

If you hit poor short game shots, chances are the bottom of the swing arc—the low point of your swing—is not in the correct place. The tendency is to impact the ground before the ball instead of hitting the ball before the ground. Here are some practice tips to make you more effective up-close.

## SHADOW DRILL

You need an old club shaft, a few balls and a sunny day for this drill. It trains you to have the bottom of your swing arc at the correct location so you can hit the back of the ball.

*1- SHADOW ON THE BACK*

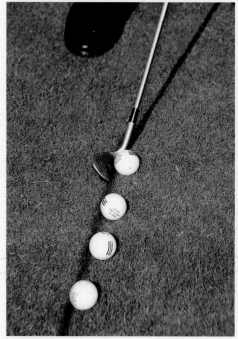

*The sun will cast a shadow from the shaft. Line up the back of the balls to the line. I'm simulating the desired impact point.*

*2- CONSISTENT SHOTS*

*Work your way down the line, training yourself to impact the back of each ball at the correct position—the bottom of your swing arc.*

*Set up the drill like this.*

# AVOID INDEPENDENT WRISTS

Wrists working independently of each other cause additional consistency problems when you're faced with trouble shots around the green. Try this drill with another line of balls to correct the problem.

*HANDS TOGETHER*

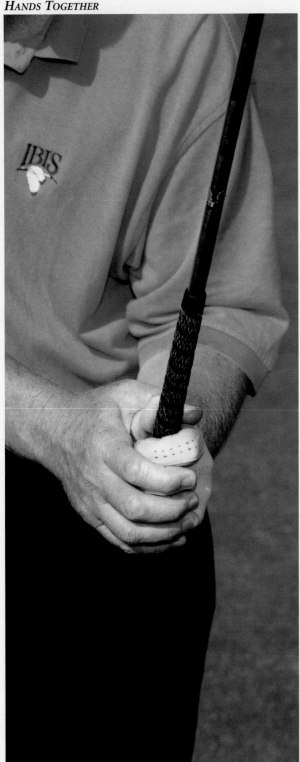

*DRAG THE LEFT HAND THROUGH*

*Place your right hand completely over your left. I suggest having a little more grip pressure on the last three fingers of the left hand.*

*Work your way down the line, dragging your left hand through each shot. You will feel your wrists working together through impact.*

Trouble
Around
the Green

# 6 GREENSIDE BUNKER TROUBLE SHOTS

*"Sand is alive. It's an evil, malevolent presence that exits solely to make golfers' lives miserable. Sand is Demon Dust."*—McMurphy's Laws of the Links

While the above may be true for some golfers, David Frost loves the sand. He even won a PGA TOUR event by playing his final two shots from bunkers. In contention at a USF&G Classic in New Orleans, his drive on the 72nd hole landed in a fairway bunker, and his next shot settled in a greenside bunker. Needing to get up and down to force a playoff with Greg Norman, David saw the line he wanted to the hole and noticed a ball mark on that line. His blast landed perfectly on the ball mark, and his ball ran in the hole for victory.

The moral of this story is that trouble shots are not really trouble shots once you learn to consistently play them. So instead of gritting your teeth and cursing the gods, play your bunker shots filled with newfound wisdom and confidence, thanks to the time you'll spend with David Frost in this chapter.

*"The most important thing about bunker play is your grip."*—David Frost

# TROUBLE SHOT:
# BASIC BUNKER TECHNIQUE

Bunker shots can be easily mastered once you understand the basic technique required to consistently get the ball out of the sand and close to or in the hole. How's that for a positive attitude? Well, becoming a good trouble shot player, in fact a good player in general, requires confidence.

The first part of this chapter demonstrates the swing required to slip the clubface under the ball, as I'm doing in the photo on this page. I'm in control, not flailing the club at the ball. The best way to begin is by showing the classic mistake that's responsible for poor bunker play. Then we'll look at my trouble-free grip, and walk step-by-step through the elements of good bunker play.

# THE BIG MISTAKE

The biggest mistake you can make is gripping your club before opening the blade. Golfers are so used to taking their grip first, it seems the natural thing to do. I'm going to teach you the correct way to avoid this error. But first, here's what the problem looks like.

**ERROR #1**

*I see my pro-am partners mistakenly grip the club first and then address the face square to the ball. Unknowingly, they have already doomed their chances for playing a good shot.*

**ERROR #2**

*Perhaps a random swing thought crosses their mind, because at this point the next mistake is opening the face of the club by turning their hands under the grip. While you need an open face to slide the clubhead under the ball, the chance of duplicating this position at impact is zero!*

# DAVID'S TROUBLE-FREE GRIP

The most important part of successful bunker play is the grip. The way you grip the club will determine how it enters the sand. The weaker the grip (the V's pointed to the left for right-handers and to the right for left-handers), the less ability the clubhead has to accelerate through the sand.

I think the stronger the grip (the V's are pointing to the right for right-handers and to the left for left-handers), the easier it is for the bounce of the club to work correctly through the sand. So take your grip using the three steps below.

## UNDERSTANDING CLUBHEAD BOUNCE

Gripping your club correctly allows the bounce of the club to work correctly through the sand. Bounce is the portion of the club that is lower than the leading edge.

### 1- OPEN THE CLUBFACE

*I open the clubface with my right hand down the shaft. Since I start my grip with the left hand, this simple step eliminates the mistake of gripping first before opening the clubface.*

### 2- LEFT-HAND GRIP

*Still holding the club with my right hand, I next position my left hand on the grip. Notice the V formed by my left thumb and forefinger is pointing toward my right shoulder (dotted line).*

### 3- SLIDE RIGHT HAND UP

*I slide my right hand up and point the V formed by that hand's thumb and forefinger toward my right shoulder. I now have an open face with a strong grip that will consistently return to this position at impact.*

Greenside Bunker Trouble Shots

# BUNKER TIPS

Before demonstrating the action sequences for playing greenside bunker shots, let's look at the key checkpoints of the swing. Consistent play comes from understanding the reasoning behind the moves.

## SHORT HAND MOVEMENT

Because you gripped the club correctly (page 119), it's easier to make the proper backswing. The key here is that your hands only move a short distance while the clubhead move a long way. The photos below prove my point.

*The backswing starts by picking the clubhead away (1) before the hands go (2). This way, the club travels parallel to the ground but the hands have moved only a short distance.*

### WRIST MOVEMENT

*My fingers indicate the very short distance the wrist cocked to bring the club parallel to the ground.*

## ARM SWING DRILL

The swing began with the simple movement of the wrists and hands bringing the club to a position parallel to the ground. This sets the correct wrist angle. The motion then switches to the shoulders and arms.

*Do this drill with only your left arm. Bring the club to parallel with a small wrist and hand movement. Then swing to the top with only your left hand on the club to develop the correct feeling. Notice the left wrist angle remains in the pre-set position.*

# BACKSWING

nlike the fairway bunker swing (around and up) you learned in Chapter 3, the greenside bunker swing is more upright. The attack angle to the ball must pull the clubhead under the sand instead of picking the ball, as we did for the fairway bunker shot.

By pre-setting your wrist angle, using only short hand and wrist movement and then swinging the club to the top, you arrive in the position you see on this page. Take a look at the clubhead, because it's a very important checkpoint. The heel of the club is higher than the toe.

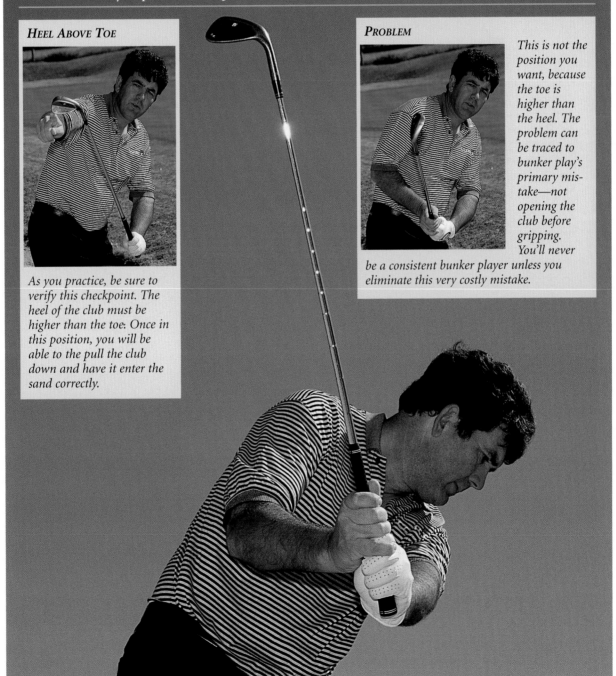

**HEEL ABOVE TOE**

*As you practice, be sure to verify this checkpoint. The heel of the club must be higher than the toe. Once in this position, you will be able to the pull the club down and have it enter the sand correctly.*

**PROBLEM**

*This is not the position you want, because the toe is higher than the heel. The problem can be traced to bunker play's primary mistake—not opening the club before gripping. You'll never be a consistent bunker player unless you eliminate this very costly mistake.*

# DOWNSWING

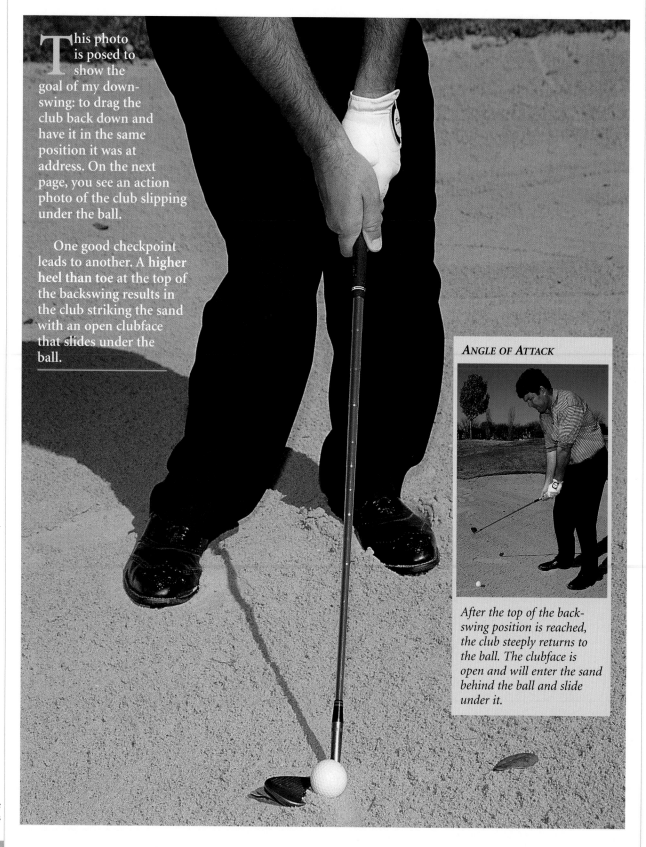

This photo is posed to show the goal of my downswing: to drag the club back down and have it in the same position it was at address. On the next page, you see an action photo of the club slipping under the ball.

One good checkpoint leads to another. A higher heel than toe at the top of the backswing results in the club striking the sand with an open clubface that slides under the ball.

**ANGLE OF ATTACK**

*After the top of the back-swing position is reached, the club steeply returns to the ball. The clubface is open and will enter the sand behind the ball and slide under it.*

# IMPACT

I posed for the photo on the facing page, but, as you can see, this one is pure action. Unlike the picking impact used for fairway bunkers, this greenside impact must have the club slide under the sand.

In this photo, it doesn't look like the ball is going anywhere because the clubhead has already passed it, but, as you'll see in the action sequences on page 124-125, the ball is headed up and out.

Greenside bunker play produces shorter, softer shots than those needed from fairway situations. The technique I've shown makes the bounce of your sand wedge work for you. The built-in bounce is the part of the club that makes it glide easily through the sand.

## INCORRECT BOUNCE

A common problem for less skilled bunker players is to feel the club bounce off the sand. The result: skulling the ball. If you open the club and then grip it correctly and follow the checkpoints I've shown, the bounce will work for you instead of against you when the clubface impacts the sand.

### FOLLOW-THROUGH

*The last checkpoint for you to look at prior to viewing the action sequences is the post-impact position of the clubhead. Notice it's still open and flatter as the club goes up toward follow-through.*

## CHECKLIST FOR BUNKER SUCCESS

✔ Open the face before gripping.

✔ A strong grip is the correct grip (V's pointing to the right shoulder for right-handers and to the left shoulder for left-handers).

✔ Begin the backswing with only a small hand and wrist movement that brings the club to a parallel to the ground position, setting the correct left wrist angle.

✔ The arms swing the club along a steeper swing plane to the top.

✔ The heel of the club must be higher than the toe at the top of the backswing.

✔ The downswing drags the club down to impact behind the ball.

✔ The club slides under the ball.

✔ The face remains open past impact. See the photo on the right for a bad example of clubface position.

*Poor bunker players have a closed face following impact. Here, the club did not slide under the ball.*

# GREENSIDE BUNKER SWING

*FACE ON VIEW SEQUENCE—GREENSIDE BUNKER SWING*

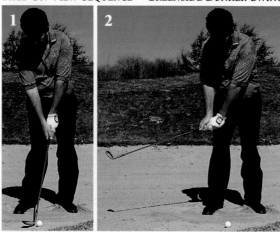

The views of my greenside bunker swing seen on this page are just as if you stood in front of me watching the swing. The views on the facing page provide a view looking from the target toward me. Notice how I achieved the very same positions and checkpoints that we featured on the past few pages.

FROM-THE-TARGET VIEW SEQUENCE—GREENSIDE BUNKER SWING

125

# TROUBLE SHOT:
# CLOSE TO LIP ON DOWNSTROKE

This downhill lie fights the ball getting airborne. The key is to adjust the ball's position in your stance. To play this shot, would you move the ball forward or back in your stance?

- Moving the ball forward will not get the ball in the air because you will hit too far behind it.

- Moving the ball back in your stance is the way to go because this shot requires a very steep downward swing to get it airborne.

### ADJUST BALL POSITION

*I've made a few adjustments from my normal bunker setup.*

*I've moved the ball back in my stance. The rake handle shows where it would normally be.*

*I'm setting the lines of my shoulders, hips and knees to match the downward slope.*

### SHAFT POSITION

*Keep your weight on your left side and pick up the shaft of the club as steeply as you can.*

*Swing the club straight down and through the ball.*

*No follow-through will occur as a result of the steep angle of attack.*

# TROUBLE SHOT:
# BALL OUTSIDE OF BUNKER

You missed the bunker, but, because you must stand in sand to get to your ball, the bunker is still causing trouble. The solution to this problem is really just two simple steps:

*1- SHOULDERS BACK*

*2- PRE-SET THE ANGLE*

*My stance looks more upright because I brought my shoulders back from the target line. As a result, my swing keeps the club outside the line to hit the ball more cleanly.*

*Guard against taking the club back to the inside. As the club returns to the ball, it will get caught up in the ground. I call that stubbing the shot.*

*To play this trouble shot correctly, your hands must be ahead of the ball at impact. My tried and true method for consistently hitting this shot with good results is to pre-set the impact angle at address (1).*

*I maintain this angle on the backswing and hold it through follow-through (2). Whenever you have a unique trouble shot, try to keep your method for playing it as simple as possible. In this case, pre-setting the angle and maintaining it through the swing ensured impact would be exactly as planned.*

# TROUBLE SHOT:
# BALL CLOSE TO UPHILL LIP

**T**his is a variation of an earlier trouble shot, where the ball was close to the downhill lip. But in this situation, with the lip looming and ready to knock the ball down, I have to adjust my setup to get the ball high quickly. This requires taking more sand, as the photo shows.

# SOLUTION: BE AGGRESSIVE

The key to playing this trouble bunker shot successfully is getting the ball up in the air as high as you can. Setting up correctly begins the process, but to be successful you must play this shot aggressively.

A ball hit from this position won't roll after landing because of the high trajectory needed to get it out quickly. Be too conservative and you have less chance for accelerating through the ball. Result: You'll have to deal with a longer putt.

### SET UP FOR THE SLOPE

My weight is on the right side. My shoulders, hips and knees are aligned parallel to the slope.

### *BACKSWING*

My weight is still on my right side. But I need some additional distance, so my backswing is more inside the line. Notice the heel of my club is higher than the toe at the top of my backswing.

### *IMPACT*

Accelerate your downswing. Hit two inches behind the ball. Notice the open clubface entering the sand.

### POWER OUT

*Seen in this close-up view, the open clubface has entered the sand behind the ball, creating a compacted sand cushion that powers the ball up and out quickly. As seen on page 128, the ball will fly high and land softly.*

Greenside Bunker Trouble Shots

# TROUBLE SHOT:
# PLUGGED LIE

The classic fried egg trouble shot! The trouble is the difficulty you'll have in getting deep enough under the ball to dislodge it from the sand in a way that will get it airborne.

I've found my best plan of attack is to use a chopping motion. As the main photo shows, chopping propels the ball up and out. Because so many shots in golf require adjustments, pros rehearse before stepping in to play them. Try this and you'll find out how quickly you focus on the technique and feeling needed to play any trouble shot successfully.

### REHEARSE THE MOTION

*To play this shot, all I do is pick the golf club up like I'm picking up an ax (left) and then dropping it straight down an inch behind the ball. I also need to program the role of my left arm on the very short follow-through. My swing key is to feel like I'm sucking my left arm behind my back (right).*

# SOLUTION: CHOP IT

These action photos show that rehearsing the shot pays. The almost straight-up backswing, chopping motion down to the ball and sucking the left arm behind my back are responsible for mastering this trouble situation. As with all trouble shots, you must practice them to gain confidence. Knowing the technique is only part of the solution. Experience is what you can really rely on in pressure situations.

*CHOP UP*

*LEFT ARM BEHIND BACK*

# TROUBLE SHOT:
# BALL BELOW YOUR FEET IN BUNKER

The trouble here is that the ball is lower than it would be if you had a flat lie in the fairway. In this case, it's about two balls lower. You could bend your shoulders over to compensate, but that's not the professional approach.

Widening my stance is the simplest adjustment to get my shoulders lower. I'm also able to hold my posture through the shot.

*Widening my stance (1) brings my chest down closer to the ball. I can maintain this posture better than just bending over at the waist. The posture remains the same at impact (2).*

*Notice how the ball is successfully climbing out of the bunker (3). I maintain this posture through the finish (4). Sometimes a simple solution is the best way out of a trouble shot situation!*

# AVOID TROUBLE:
# SELECT A LANDING TARGET

The best way to get into trouble is either to choose the wrong target or, worse yet, not have a target at all. The pin should not be your target. Here's how to select the right target:

1 Walk to the pin to get a feel of how a ball will roll after it lands.

2 Find a target about six feet forward of the hole. It should be on line with how the ball will roll after landing.

3 Program your swing tempo to land the ball on *that* spot.

Rather than shoot for the pin, select a landing target that will let the ball roll to the pin.

## KNOW THE RULES

Removing leaves, twigs or stones from around your lie in the bunker results in a one-stroke penalty. They are natural loose impediments.
—*Mark Russell*

*This shot aimed for a spot about 6 feet in front of the pin.*

# TROUBLE SHOT:
# SEVERE DOWNHILL LIES

This is similar to the bunker shot I faced when I won in New Orleans. I'm glad I did my stretching exercises the day we shot the photos on these two pages. The key to this shot is building a stable platform. That's not easy, but here are some tips:

*Your shoulders need to be closer to the ball that's below your feet. Widen your stance and open your club before gripping.*

*Buckle your knees inward to create stability. With a stable platform, your swing will be limited to your upper body.*

**3**

*Notice the heel is above the toe at the top and the blade stays open going through.*

**4**

*From this awkward position, just staying on the green is your major victory.*

Contrary to popular belief, Martin Hall thinks you struggle hitting out of the sand by taking too much sand instead of not enough. Hitting too far behind the ball is a culprit. He has a drill to help you enter the sand at the correct angle and distance behind the ball. In addition, there is a drill for helping yourself hit high, soft and short bunker shots.

## MARTIN'S RAKE DRILL

*MISS THE RAKE*

The rake provides the perfect training aid to help you enter the sand correctly. Begin by placing the ball the length of your grip away from the rake and toward the hole. The drill's goal is to swing down toward the ball so the clubhead clears the rake before entering the sand. This is the correct downward path. If it hits the rake, your path is too shallow and you are entering the sand too early.

*The clubhead travels on a downward slope that will miss the rake (1) and impact the sand the proper distance behind the ball (2). This provides the perfect amount of sand cushion needed to propel the ball out of the bunker.*

*INCREASE BALL SPIN*

*If you want to increase the ball spin, the closer you can get to the rake, the more the ball will spin. As your proficiency improves, work on entering the sand closer and closer to the rake. Compare the various results to judge the spin you created.*

# HIGH, SOFT AND SHORT BUNKER SHOT

The ominous lip of this bunker dictates the high, soft and short shot I must play. Here's a drill to help you master it.

### 1- WEAKEN GRIP

*Weaken your grip by shifting your hands so the V's formed by your thumb and forefinger point toward your left shoulder (arrows).*

*Lefthanders, to weaken your grip, your V's should point toward your right shoulder.*

### 2- TWIST THE FACE OPEN

*Pointing your left thumb toward the sky (1) twists the face of the wedge open on the backswing (2), making it easier to slide it through the sand at impact. A checkpoint is to make sure your left wrist is severely cupped during the backswing.*

## MARTIN'S SAND TIPS

Sand consistency varies, and you must adapt your technique accordingly to match the texture.

### SOFT SAND NEEDS A HARD SWING

When the sand is soft and fluffy, you need a club with a lot of bounce. My suggestion is to make a bigger swing and propel the club through the sand with a harder swing.

### HARD SAND NEEDS A SOFT SWING

You can detect the texture of the sand as you walk to your ball. If it feels hard, you can decide to use a pitching or gap wedge in place of the sand wedge. Put your weight more on your left side and limit the swing and follow-through.

Greenside
Bunker
Trouble
Shots

# 7 UNIQUE TROUBLE SHOTS

*"Golf is a puzzle without an answer. I've played the game for over 40 years and I still haven't the slightest idea how to play."—Gary Player*

**T**oday's modern courses present many unique problems for you to solve. Architects move tons of dirt, shaping and molding courses into both a beautiful and challenging test of golf.

The great proliferation of desert and mountain courses feature target golf, where you play from one green fairway sector over rocks and cliffs to the next. Sometimes the ball finds rocks, leaving you a modern version of a trouble shot.

While Mark Russell tells you about relief opportunities in Chapter 8, Ian Baker-Finch fearlessly strides into the rocks to demonstrate some interesting trouble shot solutions right here. Skip Kendall goes creekside as he plays a shot to a short tight pin. Frank Lickliter braves the winds and cold to demonstrate how to deal with weather. You'll find all of this and more in this action-packed chapter!

*"I practice trouble shots because I know I'll need them."—Skip Kendall*

*"It's one thing for someone to just tell you what to do. I'm here to show you what to do."—David Frost*

*"Trouble shots are a means to an end."—Frank Lickliter*

*"When you find yourself in trouble, the first thing to look for is getting back into the clear."—Ian Baker-Finch*

# TROUBLE SHOT:
# ROCKY DISTANCE SHOT

The Tradition is an outstanding example of why desert golf is so popular in the United States. As you can see, it makes a beautiful and challenging setting for golf. The trouble is, you may find yourself playing a lot of shots from the rocks, especially if your drives stray or you miss the green by 10 or 15 yards.

The solution to this trouble is the same whether you're hitting a long or short shot from the rocks: Strike the ball first and let the club do the work.

### 1- BRING SEVERAL CLUBS

When "climbing" in the mountains, bring a few clubs along. You never know from your cart which will be the correct club to use, so be smart and don't limit yourself to just one.

### 2- AUDITION THE CLUBS

I always mention how important it is to rehearse your shot prior to hitting it. Audition the clubs as well, picking one that's right for the job at hand. I often end up using my sand wedge, because it's not as shiny and new as the others and it won't matter if I take a little chip out of it. But for this longer shot, I've chosen a 9-iron.

### 3- BUILD A SOLID STANCE

Balance must be achieved to play these shots. I'm wedging my foot against a rock to stay in place. The ball is a little back in my stance to make it easier to hit the ball first.

### 4- PICK THE BALL OFF THE SURFACE

*I'm picking the ball off the surface, as David Frost demonstrated in the fairway bunkers. You can hardly see any material following the ball. The ball ended up on the green, and I'm acknowledging the ovation from the resident coyotes (inset).*

Unique Trouble Shots

# TROUBLE SHOT:
# ROCKY EXPLOSION

An approach shot missed the green, and here I am back in the rocks, only this time I need a softer landing shot to stay on the green and near the hole. For this shorter, 20-yard trouble shot, I'll hit a sand wedge and play it like a greenside bunker shot.

## 2- REHEARSE

## 1- CLUB SELECTION

*I pick my less-shiny sand wedge for this explosion shot.*

*Rehearsing the shot from the position you find yourself in gives you the confidence to know you won't hit a rock or cactus plant behind your ball on the backswing. You can also practice feeling your balance from your steady stance.*

# SOLUTION: EXPLODE THE BALL

There are no big rocks to ruin my club on the backswing, so I'm exploding the ball out from behind a good-sized rock in front of the ball. These are not trick shots. You can master them by adapting the techniques you've learned here.

*FOLLOW-THROUGH*

*This shot looks like a greenside bunker shot, with the sand and other material exploding the ball out of the trouble. The soil between the rocks is usually sand-based with smaller pebbles mixed in, making an explosion shot realistic.*

## REHEARSAL IS KEY!

If you think I've belabored the rehearsal idea, think back to the last televised tournament you saw where a player found himself in trouble. You saw him rehearse the shot a few times, programming his mind and muscles to adapt to the swing. It's a simple but great tip to use.

Unique
Trouble
Shots

# TROUBLE SHOT:
# CLOSE TO AN OBSTRUCTION

Boulder would be a better term for the rock this ball has found itself beside. Ian Baker-Finch is going to rehearse a shot to see how much he can bite off, using a technique you will find very helpful in similar situations, known as hooding the club.

---

*HOODING THE CLUB*

*The boulder makes it impossible for me to take the club back in a direction that will deliver the ball to the hole, so I let the club do it for me. I hood the face by slightly closing it. If I were blocked in the other direction, I would open the face.*

*NORMAL SWING TEMPO*

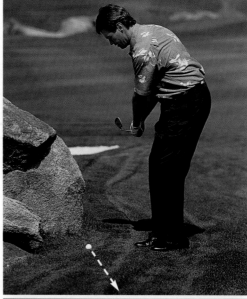

*I take the club back with my normal swing tempo, which never varies from bunker to tee. Good contact is important, so don't rush your swing. I can't adjust the swing plane to take the rock out of play. But when the hooded club impacts the ball, the clubface hooks the ball toward the target.*

# SOLUTION: HOODED CLUB CORRECTS THE STEERING

The hooded club is sending the ball on the target line to the hole. A simple solution for a seemingly difficult problem. You don't have to be in the desert to use this shot. Obstacles will creep into play on your course, and hooding or opening the club will correct the direction, if you can't take the club back on line. Practice the shot on the range by using the wooden range separators or a ball basket to block your on-target swing direction.

# TROUBLE SHOT:
# CREEK BANK TO A CLOSE PIN

Skip Kendall has two objectives here: 1) get the ball over the water; and 2) stay out of the water himself.

Water can cause problems! Ian Baker-Finch made the sports page of every newspaper in the world when he found himself in the water during the Colonial Invitational. The reason wasn't his wonderful technique for playing the shot, although he did hit a good one. He made the papers for taking off his trousers and playing the shot in his boxers.

## IAN SAYS

I had these really nice woolen trousers on. I never carried rain gear in the summer, because I was lenient on my caddies and wanted to lighten their load. I wasn't going to ruin my pants in the sticky black mud down in the water hazard.

I didn't play the shot in boxers for the publicity, but the people at Colonial said they received more publicity for that one shot than anything before or after.

### 1- SET YOUR BODY TO THE SLOPE

*Bracing myself with my lower leg so as not to fall in, I'm setting my body to the slope. I'm also choking down on my wedge and playing the shot in the middle of my stance.*

### 2- LIMIT LOWER BODY MOVEMENT

*My turn is dominated by the motion of my upper body. The lower body remains quiet. Notice how the club is in front of me, so I can control the shot.*

### 3- STAY HIGH AND DRY

*The ball is flying over the creek and will land softly on the green near the pin. I'm in balance in spite of the water hazard at my feet.*

### 4- KEEP BALANCED ON FOLLOW-THROUGH

*Even after completing the shot, my balance kept me on the land. I rehearsed the feeling before hitting the shot. I suggest you do the same as part of a regular pre-shot routine.*

Unique
Trouble
Shots

147

# TROUBLE SHOT:
# PLAYING LONG SHOTS INTO THE WIND

Frank Lickliter grew up playing in the wind, even though you wouldn't think southern Ohio is known for it. "I love playing in the wind," he says. "It requires a little more imagination, a little more thought and a little more experience."

"Sometimes it's just a hint of wind that will knock your ball down a couple of yards, if you are playing into it. The whitecaps blowing toward me in the lake along the famous 18th hole on the TPC of Sawgrass Stadium Course are real and so is the cold. Here's how to play into the wind."

*1- THINK ABOUT CLUB SELECTION*

*The windy conditions make this a 1½- to 2-club wind. This means, from a given distance, I'm going to hit two more clubs than I normally would hit. From 200 yards, I'm going to switch to a 3-iron instead of a 4-iron or 5-iron.*

*2- SETUP CHANGES*

*Normally I play a 3-iron forward in my stance (the club points to the spot), but for this shot into the wind the ball is in the middle of my stance.*

*My shoulder turn points to the golf ball. I'm not turning behind or in front of it. Ball position helps set this up. As a result, I'm not adding any tilt to my spine to make the ball get in the air. I want to stay on top of the ball.*

*Notice my left arm stays parallel to the target line and parallel to the ground at the same time. This is a restricted swing, nice and tight on top of the ball with good rotation and the visualization of keeping the ball down as it flies.*

*Keeping the ball under the wind on a lower flight trajectory allows it to gain the distance it needs to reach the green without being knocked down by the wind.*

Unique
Trouble
Shots

# TROUBLE SHOT:

# PLAYING SHORT SHOTS INTO THE WIND

The right club and a good shoulder turn can help you play short shots into the wind.

You must control ball trajectory to control the distance. Do it with club selection, ball position and a shoulder turn.

## CLUB SELECTION

With this much wind, I'll use my pitching wedge because the ball will not release very far after it hits. I'll fly it to the hole. Here are my wedges: 48½-degree pitching wedge, 52-degree gap wedge and 56-degree sand wedge.

## SHOULDER TURN CONTROLS TRAJECTORY

If you turn your shoulders so they point behind the ball, you will hit the shot higher, which I don't recommend into this wind. Turning your shoulders so they point down in front of the ball makes it easier to keep the ball down. That's the shot you want into high winds.

---

## PLAYING THE WIND

Ball position and shoulder turns work as follows:

Ball Forward + Shoulders Behind = Ball Flies High.

Ball Middle + Shoulders On Top = Ball Flies Lower.

Ball Back + Shoulders In Front = Ball Flies Even Lower.

# TROUBLE SHOT:
# THE 3-WOOD CHIP

Earlier, Frank Lickliter showed you how to play several shots when your ball is against the collar of the rough. Since this chapter is all about unique trouble shots, try this one from Skip Kendall using your 3-wood.

*1- BACKSWING*

*The mass of the clubhead means my backstroke will be very short. Notice how far I've choked down on the club to increase control.*

*2- IMPACT AND ROLL*

*The ball pops slightly up in the air as the club skims easily through the high grass at impact (1). The ball is free to roll along my selected putting line to the hole (2).*

Unique
Trouble
Shots

Coordinating rhythm and timing is extremely important when facing any trouble shot, but especially for the variety demonstrated in this chapter. The four drills Martin Hall demonstrates will all help you hit solid shots.

The confidence to hit trouble shots doesn't float around in the air. Consistently being able to hit the ball solidly from a variety of trouble lies builds the confidence needed to improve your game.

## LEFT-ARM-ONLY DRILL

### 1- LEFT HAND ONLY

*Begin by hitting shots with only your left hand. Take your normal left-hand grip as you hold the club out in front.*

### 2- POINT TO THE SKY

*Bracing your left arm below your wrist with your free right hand (inset), swing the club back to the 9 o'clock position. From this position, release through the ball with good tempo.*

## RIGHT-ARM-ONLY DRILL

To continue working on tempo and timing, repeat the one-arm drill hitting balls with only your right arm this time.

### 1- GRIP

*Grip the club as you hold it in front. Use the correct right-hand grip.*

### 2- 9 O'CLOCK BACKSWING

*Swing the club back to the 9 o'clock position. Notice how I brace the arm just below the wrist with my free left hand (inset).*

### 3- RIGHT-HAND-ONLY FOLLOW-THROUGH

*After releasing through the ball, continue on to the follow-through position, with your left hand staying as a brace. Notice I've choked down on the club.*

# LEFT-FOOT-ONLY DRILL

The coordination for hitting trouble shots is improved by drills that use only one leg at a time, much the same way as we just hit the ball one arm at a time. The key is to relax and adapt to the situation posed. Stay balanced on only the left leg, since you'll lift the right one off the ground throughout the swing.

*I play the ball back farther in my stance while addressing the ball with only my left foot on the ground (1). Staying in balance during the backswing (2) improves your overall feeling and coordination. Following through while remaining only on your left foot helps you make solid contact when playing a trouble shot (3).*

# RIGHT LEG DRILL

Working on staying in balance and feeling these various weight points during sessions on the practice range. These ideas will help you with your coordination, tempo and timing when you need them the most during a round.

*WRONG: STEEP ANGLE*

*For this drill, I don't actually raise my foot off the ground. I open the stance and place the left foot on it's toe (1). The ball is positioned in the back of my stance. Keeping the weight totally on my right foot (2), I swing back to the 9 o'clock position. My right foot continues to bear all the weight while I swing through impact to follow-through (3).*

Unique
Trouble
Shots

# 8 RULES CAN HELP YOU

*"Don't be intimidated by The Rules of Golf. They are very simple."*—*Mark Russell*

**U**nderstanding The Rules of Golf and how they apply to some of the trouble this book covers may save you strokes even before playing a shot. In some cases, you may be entitled to free relief from the trouble, while in others you may be able to escape a very bad situation by taking only a one-stroke penalty. That one stroke can look pretty good, if you're faced with what you thought was an impossible situation.

If your knowledge of The Rules of Golf, published by the United States Golf Association, is fleeting at best, or you feel intimidated by them because of the language, you're not alone. Yet, once explained, they are simple to understand and as PGA TOUR rules official Mark Russell says, "You will find the rules are there to help you."

You've seen Mark many times during tournament broadcasts, advising players on specific rules and pointing out their options, depending on the situation. All through this book, his sidebars have whet your appetite for how the rules can actually *help* you in trouble shot situations. Now it's time to dive in completely.

You may not have your TOUR card yet, but at least you will have some professional rules interpretations.

*"I think most of The Rules of Golf stink! They were written by guys who can't even break 100."*—*Chi Chi Rodriguez*

*Partners Club member Bob Yount (left) and PGA TOUR rules official Mark Russell (right) will show how some of The Rules of Golf can help you in trouble situations. Bob handles corporate marketing and sales for the Bay Hill Invitational. Mark has been a rules official for 25 years and currently is a tournament director.*

**G**olf is a lot more fun when you play by the rules. At the same time, some rules offer various forms of relief should you find yourself in a trouble situation. That's not to say you won't sometimes find yourself playing from difficult lies: Remember golf is an imperfect game.

Golf is played on the ground. Just like the pros, you're not going to get a perfect lie every time. But that's the whole essence of the game. The key is to consider the rules as part of your shot evaluation. They *may* offer a way out of trouble.

# ON THE TEE

Bob and I are on the 10th tee at Arnold Palmer's Bay Hill Club. I can assure you this tee box is in perfect condition. But should you find yourself in a situation where the ground between the tee markers is bare or damaged from everyone teeing in the same place, The Rules of Golf provide a cure.

*TEE WITHIN THE RECTANGLE*

Tee off from anywhere within this area

*Your teeing ground is really a rectangle that extends two club lengths back from and within the markers. You are entitled to play your ball from anywhere within that two-club area. The arrow indicates which direction the shot is to go.*

# TWO CLUB LENGTHS BACK

*With Mark advising (left), Bob uses The Rules of Golf to improve his tee position.*

We placed two clubs on the ground to show how much room you have to work with on the tee. Usually the grass is in better shape the farther away from the markers you get. The little distance you lose really shouldn't be a factor.

Bob has chosen to tee it up more toward the back of the tee box, but remember the rules allow you to choose any spot within that rectangular area. Choosing a good spot and hitting a good drive can help keep you out of trouble.

## WHICH CLUB TO USE

In this situation, we are using the driver to mark off the tee box distance. As the longest club in the bag, it gives the maximum relief. You'll see TOUR professionals use a driver frequently for taking relief. But you can use any club to measure.

# ADDRESSING THE BALL

I'm holding Bob's club up and away from the ground for a very specific reason. Once the ball is in play off the tee, by not grounding the club, even though he has taken his stance, The Rules of Golf stipulate that he has not addressed the ball. Should it inadvertently move, Bob will not be assessed a penalty stroke.

# AVOIDING PENALTY STROKES

*Be careful when you address this ball!*

If your ball landed in the rough and came to rest in a fluffy lie like the one at left, be very careful when you address the ball. Even though you may not have touched it, a ball can settle deeper in the grass. The Rules of Golf state that if the ball moves after you've addressed it, whether you caused it to move or not, it's a one-stroke penalty, and you must also replace the ball.

Ever wonder why Jack Nicklaus never soles his club when he takes his address? This is the reason! You can take your stance, but just don't sole your club. Below we look at the difference between a soled club and one that hasn't been soled.

## SOLED CLUB

*In this case, the bottom, or sole, of the club is touching the ground. If you have also taken your stance you are considered to have addressed the ball. Should the ball inadvertently move, you would be assessed a 1-stroke penalty and must replace the ball.*

## AVOID SOLING YOUR CLUB FOR THESE TROUBLE SHOTS

• In the rough, if the ball is sitting on top of the grass.

• When the ball is above your feet, even on the fairway.

• On loose lies.

• In a bunker, the rules prohibit soling unless it's a waste or grass bunker.

## NOT SOLED

*The box around the club and ball emphasizes that Bob has not soled his club. Instead, he is hovering it slightly above the ground. You can take your stance, and as long as you have not soled the club, if the ball moves you will not incur a penalty.*

# IMPEDIMENTS

You landed in the bunker, and your ball is resting on or surrounded by a number of objects. The question is, what type of relief from these objects will The Rules of Golf allow before you play your shot? The answer lies in understanding which objects are natural and which are man-made. The labels correctly identify them.

**Man-made Objects**
**Moveable Obstructions**
Can Be Moved

**Natural Objects**
**Loose Impediments**
Cannot Be Moved

Rule 35.

Mark your ball with a coin, ballmarker or tee when removing moveable man-made obstructions. If you did not mark your ball and it moves, and you don't know the exact spot it was in prior to the movement, the rules mandate that you must drop your ball before playing it.

You never want to have to drop your ball in a bunker!

In the bunker, you are already facing a trouble shot, so the key is getting out without incurring any needless shots or penalty strokes.

If you moved any of the natural objects seen on the opposite page, that's a penalty. A loose impediment is a natural object: a leaf, twig or stone. They **cannot be moved**.

Man-made objects—like a pencil, cigarette butt or can—are considered to be moveable obstructions, and you **can move** them.

## PLAY BY THE RULES

Two excellent books to have are *Golf Rules Plain & Simple* by Mark Russell and *The Rules of Golf* published by The United States Golf Association.

Mark's book is informative and pictorially illustrates rules interpretations in a way golfers can easily understand. You'll enjoy the game even more by playing by the rules.

Rules Can
Help You

161

# FAIRWAY RULES

Let's apply the rules for some different situations you might find yourself in with your ball in the fairway. In two cases you are entitled to relief without penalty and won't have to play a trouble shot, but in the other two you must play the ball where it lies.

Remember, golf is an imperfect game and you are not always guaranteed a perfect lie after hitting a great shot. This is exactly what makes our sport the great game that it is.

## PLUGGED LIE

Bob's ball plugged in the soft fairway, or as the rules say, it became imbedded. If you find yourself in this situation, you don't have to hit a trouble shot, because the rules allow you relief, no nearer the hole, without penalty.

The key to understanding this is that the ball has to be imbedded in its own pitch mark and must break the surface of the ground. It can't just be imbedded in the grass. If this happens to you, here's how to handle it.

### 1- REMOVE THE BALL

*Use a tee and pry up the ball. You don't need to mark the spot, since the pitch mark clearly shows the spot from where you moved it. You cannot fix the hole and replace the ball, because that would be considered improving your lie.*

### 2- CLEAN THE BALL

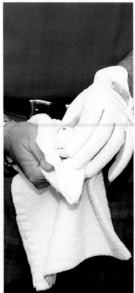

*The Rules of Golf allow you to clean your ball once it's been removed from an imbedded lie.*

### 3- DROP

*Using the ball's imbedded mark as a reference point, you are entitled to drop the ball and play the shot no nearer to the hole. The Rules of Golf helped you avoid hitting a needless trouble shot without incurring a penalty!*

# MAKE THE RULING: FAIRWAY LIES

Here are three different situations you may also encounter with your ball in the fairway. You make the ruling. Are you entitled to relief or do you have to play the shot where it lies?

*Ball in filled sand divot.*

*Ball in partially filled divot.*

*Ball resting against loose divot.*

# THE ANSWERS

If your ball was in either the sand filled or partially filled divot, you must play it where it lies. It's the rub of the green.

A divot lying in the fairway is considered to be a loose impediment and can be removed without penalty. This divot is a loose impediment because it's lying on the

fairway, whereas the partially filled divot's root structure was toward the ground. However, remove the loose divot carefully, because the rules also state that if you move a loose impediment within one club length of your ball and the ball moves, you are deemed to have caused it to move. That's a one-stroke penalty.

## RULE DEFINITION

A ball is considered to have moved when it leaves its position and comes to rest in another place. It's OK for a ball to oscillate a little because it hasn't left its position. Be careful whenever removing loose impediments within one club length of your ball!

# NEAREST POINT OF RELIEF

Bob's ball came to rest on a greenside sprinkler. The Rules of Golf have a provision to provide relief from situations where your stance, area of intended swing or ball positions are impeded, yet many golfers do not really understand the term **nearest point of relief.**

In some cases, the benefit is being able to drop the ball **without a penalty** somewhere between the nearest point of relief and a club length from it. Here's how to work with this rule, and how it can help you avoid the necessity for attempting a trouble shot.

*1- FIND THE NEAREST POINT OF RELIEF*

*The sprinkler head was in the high rough, and I'm pointing to the spot that will allow Bob to have an unimpeded stance, swing or lie. This has to be **no nearer to the hole** and it can't be out of bounds, in a water hazard or on the putting green.*

*In this case, understanding the rules will not only help Bob by removing his ball from the sprinkler head, it will also put him in a shorter cut of rough. From the point of nearest relief, you are allowed to mark off one club length in any direction, as long as it is not nearer to the hole. In this case, the club length takes him to the shorter rough and an easier shot.*

## 3- DROP THE BALL

*Bob marked the end of his club length with a red tee (circled), and now he can drop his ball between that tee and the nearest point of relief. It may be difficult to see, but the ball now lies in the shorter cut of rough.*

## HOW TO DROP THE BALL

- Stand erect

- Hold your arm straight out at shoulder level

- Drop the ball

Rules Can
Help You

# IMMOVABLE OBSTRUCTIONS

In this situation, an irrigation box is interfering with Bob's area of intended swing. While he has the skill to pop the ball up and over the box, the problem is that his club will strike the box as he follows through.

The rules allow Bob to go to the nearest point of relief where the irrigation box will not interfere with his stance, his area of intended swing or his lie. There he can drop the ball.

*Playing by the rules allows Bob to consider more options for getting his ball to where he can make a good swing, without incurring a penalty stroke. Free from the immovable obstruction, Bob now has a clear shot to the pin. Here's how we did it.*

*After Bob determined the nearest point of relief, the spot where his area of intended swing would not be interfered with, I marked the spot with a tee (inset). Always have a few in your pocket.*

### 3- MEASURE ONE CLUB LENGTH

### 4- DROP THE BALL

*Once again, Bob can drop his ball without a penalty stroke within the club length from the nearest point of relief. Now he can explore several shotmaking options for getting the ball to the pin, instead of being interfered with by an immovable object. No reason to try a trouble shot if you don't need to!*

*I'm marking off one club length from the nearest point of relief. Remember, this cannot be nearer to the hole.*

Rules Can
Help You

167

# UNPLAYABLE LIE

You can avoid a trouble shot from an extremely difficult lie by declaring it an **unplayable lie**. You will get relief from the situation, but **one penalty stroke** will be added to your score. As we look back from the green, Bob's ball is up against the root of the tree, making a backstroke impossible. A one-stroke penalty is a much better choice than attempting the shot.

## THE OPTIONS

If you find yourself unwilling to play an almost impossible trouble shot like this (and you might well be), here are some of the options to seek relief.

1 You may go back to the original point you hit the shot from and replay it. With this choice, you still receive the one-stroke penalty, but you must play the same shot you just had trouble with all over again from the same distance. This is a basic shot and distance penalty, but you can potentially save some strokes.

2 You may drop the ball within two club lengths from where the ball would lie unplayable, as long as it's not nearer to the hole.

3 Keep the point where the ball lies unplayable between you and the hole. You can go back as far as you want, as long as that point remains between you and the hole.

*HOW TO MEASURE TWO CLUB LENGTHS*

*I'm marking off two club lengths (to our left in 1 and 2, to our right in 3 and 4), no nearer to the hole, to help Bob decide which option to select.*

# DECISIONS, DECISIONS

Bob decided not to go back to the original point and replay the shot (option #1). He investigated option #2 with Mark (see how to measure two club lengths on page 168). This didn't produce good opportunities to really get back on track to the hole.

(see how to measure two club lengths on page 168)

## ALWAYS EXPLORE YOUR OPTIONS

Make it part of your strategy to explore your options before rushing into an ill-conceived shot. Playing by the rules increases your ability to strategize when faced with difficult trouble shot situations.

# THE FINAL CHOICE

Bob ended up choosing option # 3, keeping the point of the unplayable lie between him and the hole while going back as far as he wanted to. In this case, he was able to play his next shot on the tee of another hole.

*BOB'S CHOICE—GO BACK FROM UNPLAYABLE LIE*

*Playing by the rules enabled Bob to go back while keeping the point where the ball was unplayable between him and the hole. He dropped his ball on another hole's tee box. Extricating himself, using the rules related to that severe trouble shot, only cost him one stroke. Now he has an easier shot over the tree instead of a miracle shot from under the roots.*

Rules Can
Help You

# RULES FOR TREES

Before attempting a trouble shot around a tree, make sure you do not incur a penalty for improving your area of intended swing while making a practice swing. Each situation is different—as Mark's explanations point out.

In one case, you may knock down 50 leaves and not have improved your area of intended swing, while in another you receive a one-stroke penalty for knocking down just one leaf. Lets look at the differences.

## NO PENALTY STROKE

During his practice swing, even if Bob swings back and hits the limb of the tree and leaves fall down, it doesn't matter. He's done nothing to improve the area of the swing, because the limb of the tree is the problem, not the leaves. If the limb falls off, that's a different story. But even if 50 leaves fall off and the limb remains, no penalty is incurred. Remember: This rule only comes into play during practice swings.

# PENALTY SITUATION

The leaves are the area of concern. If Bob hits a leaf on his practice backswing and it falls, he's deemed to have improved his area of intended swing. Playing by The Rules of Golf, Bob would have to add a penalty stroke to his score. Golf is a sport of honor.

## KNOW THE RULES

Line of flight is never mentioned in The Rules of Golf. When anyone mentions "take it back along the line of flight," they don't know what they speak of.—*Mark Russell*

# BALL ON CART PATH

You may move your ball from a cart path without a penalty to the nearest point of relief. When you take relief, you must take complete relief. This means you do not need to be standing on the cart path or have something else interfering with your swing.

The nearest point of relief may be different for a right and left-handed golfer. Let's look at the procedure for determining Bob's closest point of relief.

## 1- DETERMINING THE NEAREST POINT OF RELIEF

*Bob is a right-handed golfer, so his nearest point of relief is behind the cart path. If he stood in front of it, his body is now between the ball and the path, extending his lie out farther. This would be lefty Phil Mickelson's nearest point of relief, but not Bob's.*

## UNPLAYABLE LIE

Calling an unplayable lie is solely up to the player. You can't take an unplayable lie in a water hazard, because in that situation you would be operating under one of the options of that hazard. But being **unplayable through the green** can be invoked as long as the player is not on the tee or green of the hole currently being played or in any of the hazards on the course. The penalty is one stroke and you must choose between the three options listed earlier as the remedy.

Trouble
Shots

172

*I've placed a tee at the point that will allow Bob to have cleared his stance, cleared the area of his intended swing and also cleared the lie of the ball.*

*Using his driver, Bob marks off one club length from his nearest point of relief. This can't be nearer to the hole. One consideration: Should the nearest point of relief be in tall rough, you may be better off hitting from the cart path.*

*Bob drops his ball without penalty within that one club length distance from his nearest point of relief. Remember, you can't end up nearer to the hole.*

*Playing by the rules allowed Bob to have a clear swing at the ball without having to attempt a trouble shot off the concrete. No penalty shot was incurred either. The rules are here to help us all enjoy the game more.*

Rules Can
Help You

# GLOSSARY

**Address** Your body position (posture, alignment, ball position) as you set up to the ball.

**Addressing the Ball** Taking a stance and grounding the club (except in a hazard) before taking a swing.

**Approach** A shot hit to the green.

**Away** A player who is farthest from the hole. This player plays his or her ball first.

**Apron** Slightly higher grassy area surrounding the putting surface. Also referred to as fringe.

**Backspin** The spin of a golf ball that is the opposite direction of the ball's flight.

**Ball Mark** The damaged, indented area in the ground caused by the ball when it lands on the green.

**Ball Marker** Something small to mark the position of your ball on the putting green. You should leave a marker when you remove your ball both to clean it and also to allow your playing partners to have an unobstructed line to the hole. Markers can be purchased and can be attached to your glove. You may also use a coin or similar object.

**Birdie** One stroke under the designated par of the hole.

**Blade** To hit the ball at its center with the bottom edge of your club.

**Blocked Shot** Hitting a ball on a straight line to the right.

**Bogey** One stroke over the designated par of the hole.

**Bump and Run** A type of approach shot that lands and then rolls onto the green and toward the hole.

**Bunker** Also referred to as a sand trap.

**Carry** How far a ball flies in the air. If a water hazard is in front of you, you have to figure the carry to be sure you've taken enough club.

**Casual Water** A temporary water accumulation not intended as a hazard. Consult the published *Rules of Golf* for information on the relief you are entitled to.

**Chili-Dip** Hitting the ground before contacting the ball. The result: weak, popped-up shots also called "fat."

**Divot** Turf displaced by a player's club when making a swing. Divots must be repaired.

**Double Bogey** Two strokes over the designated par for a hole.

**Draw** A shot that curves from right to left for right-handers and the opposite for left-handed golfers.

**Drop** The act of returning a ball back into play. Consult *The Rules of Golf* for correct information on circumstances where this occurs.

**Eagle** Two strokes under the designated par for a hole.

**Fade** A controlled, slight left-to-right ball flight pattern. Also can be called a cut.

**Fairway** Closely mowed route of play between tee and green.

**Fore** A warning cry to any person in the way of play or who may be within the flight of your ball.

**Green** The putting surface.

**Gross Score** Total number of strokes taken to complete a designated round.

**Ground the Club** Touching the surface of the ground with the sole of the club at address.

**Halved the Hole** The phrase used to describe a hole where identical scores were made.

**Handicap** A deduction from a player's gross score. Handicaps for players are determined by guidelines published by the USGA.

**Honor** The right to tee off first, earned by scoring the lowest on the previous hole.

**Hook** A stroke made by a right-handed player that curves the ball to the left of the target. It's just the opposite for left-handers.

**Hosel** The metal part of the clubhead where the shaft is connected.

**Hot** A ball that comes off the clubface without backspin and will go farther than normal as a result. If a lie puts grass between the clubface and ball, the grooves can't grip the ball to develop backspin. Understanding this, a golfer knows the ball will come out "hot" and plans for that.

**Lateral Hazard** A hazard (usually water) that is on the side of a fairway or green. Red stakes are used to mark lateral hazards.

**Lie** Stationary position of the ball. It is also described as the angle of the shaft in relation to the ground when the club sole rests naturally.

**Local Rules** Special rules for the course that you are playing.

**Loft** The amount of angle built into the clubface.

**Match Play** A format where each hole is a separate contest. The winner is the individual or team that wins more holes than are left to play.

**Mulligan** A second ball that's hit from the same location. The shot that's tried again. Limited to friendly, noncompetitive rounds.

**Net Score** Gross score less handicap.

**Par** The score a golfer should make on a given hole. Determined by factoring in 2 putts plus the number of strokes needed to cover the yardage between the tee and green.

**Provisional Ball** A second ball hit before a player looks for his or her first ball, which may be out of bounds or lost.

**Pull Shot** A straight shot in which the flight of the ball is left of the target for right-handers and right of the target for left-handers.

**Push Shot** A straight shot in which the flight of the ball is right of the target for a right-handed golfer and left of the target for a left-hander.

**Rough** Areas of longer grass adjacent to the tee, fairway green or hazards.

**Shank** To hit a shot off the club's hosel.

**Slice** A stroke made across the ball, creating spin that curves the ball to the right of the intended target for right-handed golfers and to the left of the target for left-handers.

**Stance** Position of the feet at address.

**Stroke** Any forward motion of the clubhead made with an intent to strike the ball. The number of strokes taken on each hole are entered for that hole's score.

**Stroke Play** Competition based on the total number of strokes taken.

**Target** The spot or area a golfer chooses for the ball to land or roll.

**Top** To hit the ball above its center.

# INDEX

## A

**Address**
- ball above your feet, 19, 23
- ball below your feet, 19, 20
- fairway bunkers, 43, 46
- greenside bunkers, 46
- Rules of Golf, 158–159

## B

**Backswing**
- blocked, 80–81, 91
- greenside bunkers, 120–121
- vertical, 78–79

Backward shot, 90
Baker-Finch, Ian, 6, 10, 12, 14
Ball above your feet, 19, 22–23
Ball below your feet, 19–21

**Ball position**
- close to lip on downstroke of greenside bunker, 126
- divots, 40
- high shots, 72–73
- over tree shot, 60
- playing long shots into wind, 148–149
- playing short shots into wind, 150
- practice drill for, 68
- punch shot, 99
- under trees, 62

Belly chip, 108
Blocked backswing, 80–81, 91
Blocked follow-through, 82–83
Bounce, 112
- greenside bunkers, 119

**Bunkers.** *See* Fairway bunkers; Greenside bunkers

## C

Chip shot, 81

**Clubface position**
- downhill pitch from heavy rough, 94
- draws, 66, 68
- fades, 65, 68, 76
- fairway bunkers, 43
- hook spin under tree, 74
- reverse sides, 84–85
- snagly lies, 104–105

**Clubs**
- bounce of, 112
- soling club, 23, 159

**Club selection**
- controlling downhill wedge, 88
- controlling uphill wedge, 86
- deep rough against grain, 33
- deep rough with grain, 30
- divots, 40
- downhill lie, 25
- playing long shots into wind, 148–149
- playing short shots into wind, 150
- playing wood from fairway bunker, 52–53
- punch shot, 99
- rocky distance shot, 141
- rocky explosion, 142
- uphill lie, 24

## D

**Divots**
- hitting out of, 40–41
- as loose impediment, 163

**Downhill lie**
- controlling downhill wedge, 88–89
- downhill pitch from heavy rough, 94–95
- greenside bunkers, 132, 134–135
- long game trouble, 25
- practice drills for, 36–37
- severe downhill lie to close pin, 96–97

Downswing, greenside bunkers, 122

**Draws**
- ball above your feet, 19, 23
- clubface position, 68
- draw around trees, 66–67
- shoulder position and, 69

## E

**Explosion shot**
- greenside and fairway bunkers, 45–51
- from rocks, 142–143

## F

**Fades**
- ball below your feet, 19, 20
- clubface position, 68
- fade around trees, 64–65
- low running fade, 76–77
- shoulder position and, 69

**Fairway bunkers**
- address, 43, 46
- avoiding fairway bunker lips, 54–55
- ball in bunker/stance on grass, 56–57
- ball on grass/stance in bunker, 58
- basics for, 42–43
- exploding out of, 45–51
- halfway back, 48
- impact, 51
- open clubface, 43, 44
- picking ball out of, 44
- playing wood from fairway bunker, 52–53
- pre-impact, 50
- stance on grass and sand, 59
- takeaway, 47
- top of backswing, 49

Flyer, 28
Follow-through, blocked, 82–83
Frost, David, 6, 10, 12, 14

## G

*Golf Rules Plain & Simple* (Russell), 161

**Green, trouble shots around**
- belly chip, 108
- downhill pitch from heavy rough, 94–95
- fly over hazard, 102–103
- hardpan lies, 112–113
- hitting between obstacles, 98–99
- loose lies, 110–111
- pop shot, 106–107
- practice drills for, 114–115
- putting chip, 109

- severe downhill lie to close pin, 96–97
- snagly lies, 104–105
- steep fly over, 100–101

**Greenside bunkers**
- address, 46
- arm swing drill, 120
- avoid trouble/select landing target, 133
- backswing, 120–121
- ball below your feet in bunker, 132
- ball close to uphill lip, 128–129
- ball outside of bunker, 127
- basic technique for, 118–119
- bounce, 119
- close to lip on downstroke, 126
- downswing, 122
- exploding out of, 45–51
- grip for, 119
- halfway back, 48
- impact, 51, 123
- plugged lie, 130–131
- practice drills for, 136–137
- pre-impact, 50
- sand consistency tips, 137
- severe downhill lies, 134–135
- swing, 124–125
- takeaway, 47
- top of backswing, 49

Grip, greenside bunkers, 119

## H

Hall, Martin, 7
Hardpan lies, 112–113

**Hazards**
- creek bank to close pin, 146–147
- fly over hazard, 102–103

**High shots**
- over tree shot, 60–61
- steep fly over, 100–101
- tree shots, 72–73

Hooding the club, 144–145
Hook spin under tree, 74–75

## I

**Impact**
- fairway bunkers, 51
- greenside bunkers, 51, 123

## K

Kendall, Skip, 7, 11, 13, 15
Knee shot, 91

## L

Left-arm-only drill, 152
Left-foot-only drill, 153
Lickliter, Frank, 7, 11, 13, 15
Lob shot, high, 100–101

**Long game trouble**
- avoiding trouble off the tee, 18
- ball above your feet, 19, 22–23